GROW GREAT VEGETABLES IN
Michigan

GROW GREAT VEGETABLES IN
Michigan

Edited by Bevin Cohen

TIMBER PRESS
Portland, Oregon

To Heather, Elijah, and Anakin. Thank you for always being there with me in the garden of life.

Frontispiece: Few things are more rewarding than harvesting homegrown vegetables from one's own garden.

Copyright © 2023 by Timber Press. All rights reserved. Based on *Vegetable Gardening in the Midwest* by Michael VanderBrug, edited by Bevin Cohen.

Front cover photos by (clockwise from top left): Stephen Ausmus, USDA ARS; PxHere (CC0 License); iStockPhoto/sagarmanis; iStockPhoto/Eugenegg
Back cover photos by: iStockPhoto/AlexRaths (top); iStockPhoto/FatCamera (bottom)
Illustrations © Julia Sadler and Juliana Johnson.
Interior photography and other illustration credits appear on page 201.

Published in 2023 by Timber Press, Inc. a subsidiary of Workman Publishing Co., a subsidiary of Hachette Book Group, Inc.
1290 Avenue of the Americas
New York, New York 10104
timberpress.com

Printed in China on responsibly sourced paper.
Text design by Sarah Crumb.
Cover design by Amy Sly and Adrianna Sutton.

ISBN: 978-1-64326-156-0
A catalog record for this book is available from the Library of Congress.

CONTENTS

PREFACE

By gardening in Michigan—land of vast plains, rolling hills, rivers, and lakes—you are participating in a long and complex agricultural history. This region's fertile soils make it second only to California in terms of the diversity of plants you can grow. Cool-season crops such as lettuce, peas, asparagus, potatoes, and cauliflower flourish in our chilly, damp springs. With the long, hot summers in most areas, beans, tomatoes, eggplant, corn, and other warm-season crops are possible. In fact, you can grow virtually any vegetable, from arugula to zucchini. Even winter, tough as it may be, is a boon to the gardener. The cold temperatures have a sanitizing effect on our gardens, helping to minimize the inevitable pests and diseases. And cold months give us some time to reflect, regroup, and start planning for an even better season next year. This is the good news.

Gardening in Michigan has its challenges, too, in the form of harsh winters, summer droughts, unpredictable storms, and weeds, which love our rich soils as much as the vegetables do. This book will show you how to mitigate many challenges through preparation and patience. Of course, sometimes there is nothing to do when a windstorm blows down your tomato trellis, or a torrential downpour floods the entire garden. But for me, this is part of the excitement. Time outside of our normal routines—and just plain outside— exposes us to the elements and heightens awareness of our surroundings. Although the seasons are relatively predictable, what happens within each one is not. On more than one occasion I have harvested crops in

a hailstorm, transplanted in the rain, and pulled carrots out of frozen soil. Gardening requires dedicated observation as every year brings new trials, surprises, and successes.

I was born in Michigan and now reside less than a half hour from where I was raised, roughly in the middle of the lower peninsula. I have enjoyed gardening for most of my life and for the past decade or so, have been lucky enough to be able to visit communities across the state to share my knowledge, my experience and, of course, my seeds. Michigan is full of different microclimates, each with its own peculiarities, and I think that's part of what makes gardening fun.

Each garden is unique to its location, and unique to its gardener. We each bring a different perspective to our work and, in turn, our gardens reflect who we are. This is one of the great joys of gardening. It is your space, and you can decide what you want to grow, how big the garden is, or if you feel like weeding today or not. No garden is perfect, but the one you create is all yours. Over time you will get to know your specific growing area and soil, and slowly become the expert on your garden space like no one else ever could be. Use this book as a guide, and then observe, experiment, taste, and dig in. Above all, savor the spicy arugula, the sun-warmed heirloom tomatoes, the colorfully patterned beans, and the pure joy of digging up perfect fingerling potatoes. You are in Michigan, and you can grow just about anything!

—BEVIN COHEN

ACKNOWLEDGMENTS

I have been gardening for many years but it wasn't until recently that I was encouraged to pick up a pen and begin writing about my experiences in the garden. Through gardening we can learn so much: about nature, about the food we eat, and maybe most importantly, about ourselves.

I've now written dozens of articles and published a number of books about gardening, herbalism, seed saving, and storytelling. Perhaps it is the stories that excite me the most. The stories that we tell as we shell beans together on the back porch, or while we transform a bountiful harvest into a flavorful meal.

Thank you to all my gardening friends that have shared their seeds and their stories with me. You've passed along more than just next year's plantings. You've let me in on your triumphs and challenges, your wisdom and your humor. As each season has passed, my gardens have thrived because of your generosity.

Thank you to Timber Press for allowing me this opportunity to pass along my experiences and to share my stories through these pages. As our gardens grow, we also grow as people. Through the uncertain weather of life, we persevere and together we enjoy an abundant harvest.

Get
Started

Do Michigan-grown tomatoes like this one have better flavor? Find out for yourself by growing your own.

WELCOME TO GARDENING IN
Michigan

Michigan has a long and celebrated history of agriculture. This great state is the second most agriculturally diverse in the nation and Michigan farmers produce more than 300 different types of food and agricultural products. We're relatively far from the temperature-moderating effect of the oceans, so we can all agree that winters are typically cold and summers are hot and humid. But within those basic parameters, a broad spectrum of growing circumstances awaits us thanks to large-scale microclimates (topography, bodies of water, urban versus rural areas) and those on the small scale in your yard. In order to begin planning, it is important to first understand where your garden fits in our state's overall climate, and narrow it down from there.

◄ Heirloom vegetable patch at Michigan's Farm Garden at the Frederik Meijer Gardens in Grand Rapids.

Understanding Our Climate

As gardeners, we are subject not only to weather but also to climate. Where we live informs what we can grow and for how long. To assess how your climate will affect your growing season, this book uses the plant hardiness zone map from the United States Department of Agriculture (USDA). The map is based on average annual minimum winter temperatures and each zone represents a difference of 10 degrees F. The map was originally published in 1960 and was most recently updated in 2012, using more detailed data from the previous 30 years. Michigan includes USDA climate zones 4 to 6, which is a rather broad spectrum of growing circumstances.

In addition to knowing your climate zone, crucial knowledge for any gardener is the length of the growing season, or when you can expect the season's first and last frosts. First frost arrives in fall and knocks out the tomatoes and basil, whereas last frost is the date in spring after which you can begin to plant tender, heat-loving crops like eggplants. The crops you grow will require different numbers of days to mature to a useful size. There is nothing worse than bearing witness to a beautiful Brussels sprout stalk that hasn't had enough time to actually form the sprouts. Knowing the length of your season will motivate you to plant on time. This information will also help you decide what varieties to choose or if you should simply skip some crops. Remember that hardiness zones are based on averages, so in cases of extreme cold or heat, prepare to assist your plants. As a gardener, you will pay closer attention to forecasts than non-gardeners. It is particularly critical to pay attention at the beginning and end of the season and have your emergency plans in place, such as row covers or old sheets for frost protection or a sprinkler to cool off sweltering crops.

The best source I've found for first and last frost dates is the Farmers' Almanac website. I've compiled a few cities in each hardiness zone on the frost-date chart; look for a city near you as a starting point for understanding the length of your growing season. Remember that frost dates can vary significantly, even within one city. Search local gardening forums or call your extension office for more specific dates.

MICROCLIMATES

As you become familiar with your hardiness zone and average frost dates, remember that these guidelines may not accurately reflect your own tiny piece of earth. Proximity to bodies of water, hills and valleys, or urban areas can result in large-scale microclimates—variations in climate from the surrounding area—within a particular zone.

MICHIGAN HARDINESS ZONES

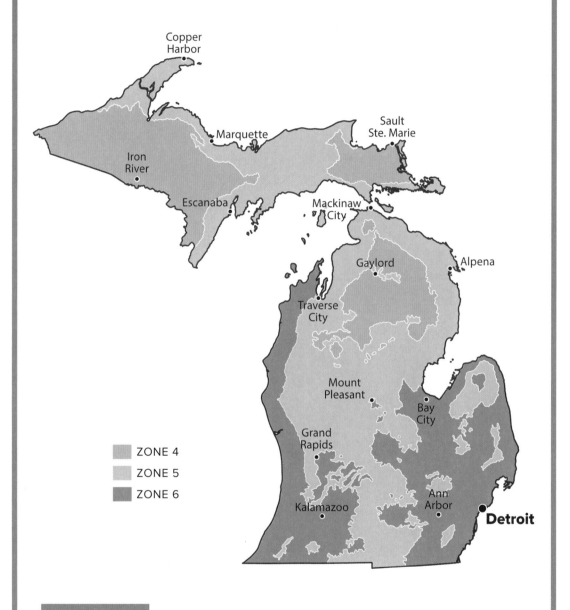

Copper
Harbor

Sault
Ste. Marie

Marquette

Iron
River

Escanaba

Mackinaw
City

Gaylord

Alpena

Traverse
City

Mount
Pleasant

Bay
City

Grand
Rapids

ZONE 4
ZONE 5
ZONE 6

Kalamazoo

Ann
Arbor

Detroit

Michigan covers hardiness zones 4 to 6. Knowledge of average temperature ranges and frost dates helps gardeners estimate the length of their growing season.

AVERAGE FROST DATES IN MICHIGAN

CITY OR AREA	FIRST FROST	LAST FROST	FROST-FREE DAYS
Iron River	September 3	June 14	80
Copper Harbor	October 15	May 10	147
Marquette	October 13	May 11	154
Escanaba	October 10	May 10	152
Sault Ste. Marie	September 25	May 28	119
Mackinaw City	September 14	May 29	107
Traverse City	October 1	May 29	124
Alpena	October 12	May 6	158
Gaylord	September 19	May 27	114
Bay City	October 12	April 30	164
Mount Pleasant	October 10	May 4	158
Grand Rapids	October 8	May 5	155
Kalamazoo	October 11	May 4	159
Ann Arbor	October 15	April 28	169
Detroit	October 23	April 22	183

The microclimate, which may extend for miles, can mean changes in temperature (warmer or colder), precipitation (wetter or drier), or likelihood of frosts (more or less prone) on either end of the season.

Large bodies of water like the Great Lakes, for example, tend to moderate the air temperature of nearby areas; smaller bodies of water will have the same effect, but often on a lesser scale. This means gardens may be less likely to experience extreme low temperatures or frosts in late spring and early fall, but more likely get slammed with lake-effect snow (produced by the interaction between the warmer water temperature and the cold winter air). Because cold air is heavier than warm air, if you garden in a valley, you may experience more frost than someone living on top of a hill. As an example, the elevation of the land I farm is around 20 feet lower than the neighborhood where I live next to the farm. When I hear an overnight temperature of 40°F predicted for the nearest city, I know that it is possible I will see frost on the farm, as an 8- to 10-degree difference can easily exist between the house and the farmland. Your microclimate could potentially mean a difference of 2 to 3 weeks in your growing season as compared to the surrounding area, which is a significant factor in what you can plant and when.

If you live in the city surrounded by other homes or buildings, you may experience slightly warmer temperatures than if you gardened in surrounding exposed, rural areas. This is because buildings and paved areas will often absorb heat during the day, which is then released into the air at night. In colder times of the year, this could mean potentially reducing the chances of frost—but in summer it might result in trapped heat and scorched plants. Certain buildings or fences may protect your plants from wind or create wind tunnels.

You can't do much about the large-scale microclimates that affect your garden beyond incorporating that awareness into your plant selection and timing. But it is smart to take advantage of (or modify when possible) small-scale microclimates that you observe in your yard, such as structures that block the sun, walls that reflect heat, or areas of high wind exposure. Keeping records and paying close attention are critical.

GROWING DEGREE DAYS

A calculation that may turn out to be just as helpful as the number of frost-free days is the measurement of heat accumulation expressed as growing degree days (GDD). In other words, it is not just the length of season that matters; it is the accumulated heat within a season that informs when crops will ripen. Although you may have 140 frost-free days in a season, those days are not equal. As the day length shortens in the fall and temperatures drop, plant growth significantly slows down. The same is true for the early spring. It is especially important to consider GDDs when growing fruiting and heat-loving crops. Tomatoes, for example, require 1500 GDDs, which on average will take until around the end of July in lower Michigan to reach that number. This makes sense logically. It is the total amount of heat that drives the growth. If you have a week of really warm weather and then a week of unseasonably cold weather, you will see significant differences in the amount of growth during those weeks. This is a reminder that it is critical to get those crops in on time—or early if you can protect them—so you'll actually see the fruits of your labor.

To calculate the GDD, you must first know the base temperature for your crop. This number represents the lowest temperature at which the plant will grow. This will vary depending upon the species. For example, the base temperature of tomatoes is 50°F. Tomatoes simply won't grow at temperatures lower than this. Once you know the base temperature of your crop, you'll need to calculate the mean temperature for the day. This can be done by simply adding the highest temperature of the day with the lowest and then dividing by two. Now, take the mean temperature of the day and subtract the base temperature of the crop to determine the Growing Degree Day (GDD) value.

Growing in the Great Lakes Region

- Zones: 3 to 7
- Growing season: 130 to 180 days
- Average precipitation: 35 inches

The Great Lakes region includes all the states in the Midwest that touch a Great Lake: Wisconsin, Michigan, Illinois, Indiana, and Ohio. This area has some of the most unpredictable weather because of the lakes' influence over the region. But those lake waters also moderate the temperature and bring moisture inland, allowing for fruit production, which now includes a thriving wine industry. The glacial history provides a huge variety of fertile soils and more rainfall than is typically seen in the Central Plains. This allows for many different vegetables and fruits to be grown in the region. In the northernmost areas you may have difficulty ripening fruits, as in the Northern Plains. A hoop house or row cover system will be beneficial.

IS IT WORTH THE RISK?

Once you have figured out your place in the region and what your frost-free window looks like, get to know what sort of gardener you are when it comes to pushing the seasons. For my region and specific microclimate, I have settled on October 15 as the first frost date and May 15 as my last frost date, although these dates aren't set in stone and certainly vary from year to year. I could push the season a little on either end, but I am not the farmer who tries to have the first tomatoes at market. Fellow gardeners in my neighborhood show me their red, ripe tomatoes with proud smiles on their faces weeks before I harvest mine. They took the risk and they get the bragging rights—I am okay with that.

So, are you a risk taker or are you more conservative? Figure out your frost dates and decide if you want to push the seasons. If you are into taking risks, go for it. Sometimes those bragging rights are worth it! Some ideas on how to extend the season are provided later in this book.

◀ A hoop house can help you get started earlier and extend the season, amidst sometimes unpredictable Midwest weather.

GARDENING 101

When I talk to new gardeners, I often encounter a wall of fear and intimidation. Gardening seems to have so many rules and the fear of failure runs high. Some people have been burned by first experiences, like that spider plant they killed in their first apartment or those daffodil bulbs that never emerged from the soil. They imagine gardening as something only for those born with green thumbs—some mysterious ability given only to the luckiest people. I am here to state for the record that this is false. Anyone can learn to be a gardener.

◀ Growing veggies means getting to know your soil.

Some of this fear is related to how disconnected our lives have become from the natural processes and cycles that are going on around us all the time. That tree growing in a cement crack alongside the building you walk past every evening? It was once just a seed that found fertile-enough soil to grow; no need for some fancy-pants gardener with the newest ergonomic tool or the best soil amendments on the market. Participating in gardening is a decision to get involved in the natural world, and part of this involvement is learning how to trust nature. Once we have that trust, we can let go and really start growing. Plants want to grow—we are just here to assist them!

Remember that bean seed you grew in a Styrofoam cup in elementary school? That was gardening. Sun, nutrient-rich soil, water, and a seed are all you need.

Sun and Shade

An important factor in deciding where to locate your garden is sunlight. Sun is what gives plants life, stimulating growth and the production of fruit. All annual vegetable plants prefer full sun. This will allow them to grow faster, produce fruit reliably, and fully mature into plants with bright colors and sturdy stems. But I know full sun is not always possible, and I don't suggest cutting down the beautiful shade trees in your yard just so you can grow tomatoes. If you really want to grow tomatoes and you don't have enough sun, a community garden plot is a good option to pursue. But first, try to assess the amount of sun you have.

Full sun is defined as 6 or more hours of direct sunlight. Between 4 and 6 hours of full sunlight is defined as partial sun, while 2 to 4 hours is partial shade. Moving toward 2 hours (or less) of direct sun per day puts you in the full shade category, an unlikely environment for the survival of edible plants. A lot of nuance exists in these categories when you consider the filtered sun through leaves and fencing, along with the time of year and the difference between morning and afternoon sun. As you choose where to establish your garden, note which way is south, and locate anything that might cause shading like trees, your house, or the neighbor's house. If you can, spend a day observing your gardening space, preferably in the spring when the sun gets a little higher. Every hour or so note the lighting conditions.

In my experience, it becomes difficult to grow fruits like peppers and tomatoes with any less than 5 hours of sun. I have grown cherry tomatoes in 4 to 5 hours of sun, but they take significantly longer to mature and I don't feel like they are quite as sweet. If your garden gets less than 4 hours of sun, focus on shorter-season crops such as arugula, chives, cilantro, parsley, scallions, kale, and other

◄ **Cherry tomatoes can get by with 4 to 5 hours of sun, but they take longer to ripen.**

leafy greens. You will notice that colors are less vibrant with less light and flavor profiles may change. Sun assists all functions of a plant, including the production of sugar and spice, making hot peppers less hot and snap peas less sweet. Although some shade can be challenging, don't be deterred: experiment, learn, and have fun.

Soil Types

Soil is a living organism and the basis for your success as a gardener. When treated poorly, soil can go dormant or die, but it will support life when fed and active. The basic components of soil are organic matter (leaves, compost, or anything that once lived), minerals, microbes, and water. Air is also critical for the root systems of plants, which need to breathe just like all living organisms. The amount of space between the particles in your soil determines what type of soil structure or texture you have: sand, silt, clay, or loam.

▪ **Sandy soils** are high in minerals, but tend to be naturally low in organic matter and nutrients because they drain too well. As water moves swiftly through sandy soils, it washes away any existing nutrients. Add organic matter to sandy soils to improve its moisture-holding ability and increase nutrient availability.

▪ **Clay soils** hold moisture, but the fine particles form a virtually impenetrable surface, leaving little room for air and preventing drainage. The good news is that clay soils are generally chock-full of minerals and quite fertile. You just need to add organic matter to open up the soil, allowing air and water to pass through. Planting cover crops like rye biologically encourages aeration by creating openings in the soil wherever the cover crops' roots go. Mulching also encourages insects and worms, which are some of the best aerators.

▪ **Silt** is made up of very small particles of the minerals quartz and feldspar with a texture between sand and clay. It is the stuff that has made river floodplains so rich and attractive for farming. Silt also allows for good drainage.

▪ **Loam**, the ideal, contains some sand, some clay, and some silt, giving you the benefits of all those materials. Loamy soils drain well but still retain water, and have good aeration and excellent bacterial activity.

Assessing your soil means not being afraid to get your hands dirty.

Feeding Your Soil

Although most soil contains a diversity of nutrients, those nutrients will be depleted over time as plants are harvested. Soil that is used repeatedly to produce food pushes the natural system to its limits and must be cared for constantly. Adding an array of nutrients in balance is critical to healthy soil that will produce nutritious and flavorful food. And no matter what soil type you have, consistent applications of organic matter (and compost in particular), will literally feed your soil, providing food and energy for the invisible activity that is always happening in good soil conditions.

The three basic nutrients that plants need are nitrogen (N), phosphorus (P), and potassium (K). Nitrogen is the impetus for growth of a plant's foliage; phosphorous promotes growth of flowers, fruits, and strong roots; and potassium is connected to general plant health and balanced growth. You will see three numbers listed on almost any fertilizer package; these indicate the percentage of each element in the fertilizer mix, always in the order of N-P-K. Micronutrients such as calcium, magnesium, sulfur, iron, and zinc are also critical. As with human health, diversity is a powerful ally in our gardens. The broader the palate, the better chance we have at fighting off disease, and increasing our health, the health of our plants, and the health of our soil.

Synthetic or inorganic fertilizers tend to have higher numbers than organic fertilizers. With heavy doses of a few elements, inorganic fertilizers promote fast growth and can provide significant yields, but they also bypass the more nuanced and holistic approach of soil health. Plants fed with inorganic fertilizers tend to lack flavor and be less nutritious. Organic fertilizers, on the other hand, release nutrients more slowly (so plants receive a steadier supply of food), and they improve your soil over time. A balanced all-purpose

DIY SOIL COMPOSITION TEST

This simple test will show you the rough proportions of sand, silt, and clay in your soil, offering general guidance on your soil's ability to hold water and nutrients. Combine this activity with a test of your soil's nutrients and you will be well on your way to a deeper understanding of the material in which your vegetables are growing.

YOU WILL NEED:

- Quart-size glass jar with a lid

- Trowel

- Soil sample

- Water

▲ Know the percentage of sand, silt, and clay in your soil, and you can estimate its water- and nutrient-holding ability and determine what needs improving.

STEPS:

1. Collect enough soil to fill your jar halfway. To represent your garden well, collect soil from several different areas and mix them together. Gently push aside surface debris, and avoid grass, mulch, and stones.

2. Add water until the jar is three-quarters full.

3. Place the lid on the jar and shake vigorously until all chunks of soil have broken down.

4. Set the jar in a visible location and observe. After a few days, you should be able to see the formation of layers in your jar. Sand, the heaviest particles, will settle on the bottom, the next layer will be silt, and then clay. The organic matter will float to the top of the water.

organic garden fertilizer is a good choice for general use. If you are feeding the soil with everything from manganese to zinc, providing a foundation, the plants will decide when and how much of each nutrient they need. That said, some crops need higher ratios of certain elements; corn, for example, benefits from applications of extra nitrogen. Get to know the needs of your crops and watch for signs of deficiencies such as yellowing leaves or stunted growth.

A smart place to start figuring out exactly what your soil needs is to do a soil nutrient-level test. You can do a simple home test, send it away to a lab, or bring a soil sample to your local cooperative extension agent. I highly recommend professional insight, especially at the beginning. For years, I used a soil consultant for my testing who would go over the results with me, explain the critical parts, and make recommendations. Once you know more about your soil, you can find specific organic amendments (such as greensand, alfalfa meal, or fish meal) that will target what your soil is lacking. It is not only about amending with the right material, but getting those nutrients to be active in the soil system. You should add most amendments in the fall to give your soil a chance to digest the amendments before you plant again in the spring. Nitrogen is the exception; because it moves through the soil a lot faster, you should add it in the spring. Feeding the soil is an ongoing process of building and balancing.

SOIL PH

Soil pH, a measurement of the acidity or alkalinity of soil, is a vital part of feeding your soil because plants can only access nutrients if the soil is within a specific range. If the pH of your soil is out of that range, nutrients won't dissolve, meaning they will never become available to your plants, and plants will starve. Along the pH scale of 0 (most acidic or sour) to 14 (most alkaline or sweet), the ideal pH for vegetables is within the range of 6 to 7.5, with 6 being fairly acidic and 7.5 being more alkaline. A pH of 7 is neutral. This shows that plants are generally more tolerant of acidic soils than they are of alkaline soils.

Areas that get less rain tend to be more alkaline, whereas rainy areas are often more acidic, because rain tends to wash calcium and other nutrients from the soil. Fortunately, soils in the Midwest tend to have a neutral pH that is perfect for growing fruits and vegetables. This doesn't mean you shouldn't pay attention, however, because chances are your soil will still need amending, particularly soil around your house that has been trucked in, or soil that you bought to fill raised beds.

To find out your garden's soil pH you must test it. Many pH testing kits are available online or at garden centers, although the results are often less than accurate. Again, I recommend sending your soil (contact your local extension office or research soil-testing labs) for a complete nutrient-level test that includes pH. You will learn exactly what your soil needs and find out how to balance your soil. The common response to a low or high pH result is to amend the soil with lime (to raise the pH) or sulfur (to lower the pH). Sometimes these amendments will help balance your soil significantly, but occasionally it may be more complicated. For example, one field on my farm consistently had a pH around 7.5. Significant calcium deposits existed near the surface of the soil, and yet there was not much available calcium in the soil for the plants to use because the other nutrients were out of balance. For several years my soil consultant recommended adding calcium to the soil, in order to get the available and active nutrients in balance, with the hope that the soil would begin to use up the nearby calcium deposits and make them available. It was counterintuitive to add calcium to soil with a high pH, but that's what was needed to get the nutrients in the soil balanced.

Compost Basics

Composting is a simple, natural process of breaking down organic materials into a concentrated and nutritious material that does wonders for soil health, especially in intensive garden spaces. I am a pretty lazy composter, so I often take advantage of anaerobic composting—piling up my garden waste and allowing it to decompose naturally with perhaps an occasional turn or two. On the flip side, active, or aerobic, composting requires more attention to get the right balance of carbon-rich (brown) and nitrogen-rich (green) materials. Although the process is fairly simple, a few guidelines will help you succeed.

LOCATION

The location of your compost pile is the first consideration. Moisture balance is important, so choose a site with at least some shade if possible. The site should be convenient to both your kitchen (so you can easily carry kitchen scraps to the compost) and your garden (so you can haul the compost when it is finished). An accessible water source is also helpful in case you need to add water.

TYPE AND SIZE

The type and size of your compost pile will be determined by how you want to use it and what materials you will be adding. A classic

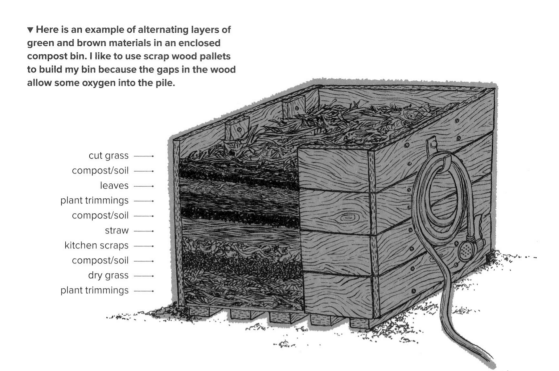

▼ Here is an example of alternating layers of green and brown materials in an enclosed compost bin. I like to use scrap wood pallets to build my bin because the gaps in the wood allow some oxygen into the pile.

cut grass ⟶
compost/soil ⟶
leaves ⟶
plant trimmings ⟶
compost/soil ⟶
straw ⟶
kitchen scraps ⟶
compost/soil ⟶
dry grass ⟶
plant trimmings ⟶

compost heap, which should eventually be at least 3 feet wide by 3 feet high, works well if you have a large amount of material to add. At this size, the heap will be large enough to "cook," heating up enough to kill weed seeds and various diseases. You can literally just pile the materials or you can build a simple enclosure to hold the materials in place. I recommend using slats, or some type of durable screen so that air can get into the pile more easily and it can release excess moisture if needed. Another simple method is to stack a couple of straw bales as walls, which is also a convenient way to keep carbon materials nearby to add to your pile.

A compost tumbler effectively composts smaller quantities of material, and faster. It will also keep unwanted pests from scavenging out of your compost pile. Tumblers are available in different sizes and styles, and they usually come with specific instructions that include tumbling your compost frequently. These composters make turning your compost effortless. Shredding your dry materials will allow you to fit more material in your tumbler and it will break down more quickly, giving you compost sooner.

MATERIALS

Effective composting requires adding balanced quantities of green nitrogen-rich materials and brown carbon-rich materials. As the green materials digest the brown materials, compost is made. A good rule of thumb for ratios is one part green material to two parts brown material. Common green materials are cut grass, vegetable trimmings and kitchen scraps, manure, eggshells, tea bags or tea leaves, and coffee grounds. Common brown materials are straw, dry grass, leaves, and paper. I tend to avoid wood chips and sticks because they are much harder to compost and use a ton of nitrogen to break down. Never compost meat or bones, dairy, fish, human or pet waste, diseased plants, seeding weeds, or inorganically treated plants. I like to layer the green and brown materials like lasagna, adding thin layers of soil or finished compost to inoculate the soil with microbes and get the compost moving in the right direction.

TURNING AND WATERING

Turning your compost frequently is important, especially with a larger pile, because it allows air into the composting process. And as with a fire, the oxygen will fuel the process. Often, the pile will noticeably warm up immediately after turning. A good digging fork usually works best because it allows you to penetrate the pile more easily. Turning also allows you to see your compost and potentially make adjustments. If it is soaking wet and slimy, add more brown. If it seems dry, add water. If the pile has too much brown and nothing is happening, add more green. You can usually tell from the sour smell, or from no smell, if the compost does not have enough food and it stops forming. Finished compost (the pile should be ready in a few months to a year, depending on the size and how often you turn it) will be dark and crumbly and smell earthy and fresh.

Water

Providing your plants with sufficient water is another important consideration. The trick is to not overwater, while still giving plants enough water to thrive. The general rule of thumb is that plants should receive about an inch of water per week, so that means the amount of rainfall you are getting will affect how much you need to irrigate.

How soil holds or is able to drain water depends on its composition and how you care for it. Sandy or rocky soils with fast drainage may need more water. A friable, non-compacted soil with a higher percentage of organic matter will be able to retain moisture better (important in July!).

Observation is key. Stick your hands in the soil and if the soil is moist 1 or 2 inches down, you are in good shape; if it is dry a few inches down, you probably need to water. Some plants, like broccoli and squash, will wilt a little during the hottest times of the day to conserve energy and cool down. However, for most plants, significant wilting indicates that plants need water.

Too much or too little water can also show up as yellowing of the leaves. This brings us to the most common problem: too much water. It is certainly true that plants need water to grow, but too often we equate more water with more growth. In fact, too much water is just as bad as too little. If you have in-ground sprinkling near your garden, I recommend putting it on its own separate zone so that it doesn't turn on every day. Keep a close eye on your plants and they will tell you when you are on the right track.

WATERING METHODS

Water is essential to gardening—that's a fact. But the way you choose to deliver water to your garden will depend a lot on your soil, what you are growing, and the size of your garden.

◀ **A watering can with a removable rose comes in handy for many gardening tasks.**

Sprinklers. The best thing about sprinklers is that they are flexible—you can move them, turn the water pressure up or down, and put them on timers. You can choose among many sprinkler styles, each with an advantage for a specific context and use. For example, oscillating sprinklers deliver a soft, gentle spray for newly planted crops in open areas without low branches. For more established crops, impact sprinklers deliver a powerful spray in a circle low to the ground. Rotary sprinklers, which move gently in a circle, work well in large, open gardens. It is important to know how sprinklers function so you can get even coverage. If you aren't sure how much water a sprinkler is putting down (and where), place a few small buckets near the plants as gauges. With any type of sprinkler, evaporation can be an issue, so water on cloudy days when possible.

Soaker hoses or drip irrigation. The main advantages to a soaker hose (which is simply a porous hose) or a drip irrigation system is that less water is lost to evaporation, and the foliage is kept dry, which reduces disease. I have used soaker hoses for urban shade gardens, greenhouse tomatoes, and coiled up as a cooling system for midsummer hot houses. Use garden staples to hold them in place, and if you are mulching, set up the hoses underneath. Soaker hoses are easier to find in local hardware stores. Look for drip systems, which require a little more technical ability and planning, in gardening catalogs.

Watering cans. Although not a practical way to water the entire garden, watering cans are great for certain tasks like watering pots, small plantings, and areas missed by a sprinkler. You can also use watering cans to deliver diluted fertilizer to your transplants. I prefer a can with a removable rose. The rose creates a light stream of water, which is excellent for watering young seedlings. But it's also nice to have the ability to pour water quickly if desired and it's easier to clean out the watering can if you can remove the rose.

WATERING WITH RAIN

In most areas of the Midwest, summers consist of dry spells with occasional thunderstorms. I have spent many moments staring at the radar, praying that a lone thunderstorm crossing Lake Michigan builds strength and unloads its stored energy on my farm in the form of rain. Any water is welcome when it is hot and dry, but the downside of a thunderstorm, as opposed to a steady rainfall, is that the water comes so hard and fast that the soil can't soak it all up. By connecting your gutter system to a rain barrel, you can save some of that excess water to use in the garden later. Storing rain is by no means a new idea, but the rain barrel is an accessible and simple technology for home gardeners. You can build your own rain barrel or purchase one that is ready-made.

Most homes could easily fill two or three 55-gallon barrels. (Just one inch of rain on a 1000-square-foot house, for example, will yield 600 gallons!) Equip rain barrels with tight-fitting covers so they don't fill up with leaves, become breeding grounds for mosquitos, or serve as death traps for small rodents or birds. Remember: you are harvesting the perfect (free) water for your plants—without chlorine and other additives of municipal water—so you want to keep it clean. Fill up your watering can or connect a gravity-fed hose to the spigot at the bottom of the barrel to easily deliver water to your garden.

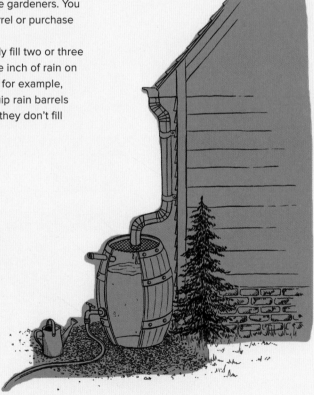

▶ Rain barrels are great ways to conserve water during the hotter months. Support the barrel with a level and stable base.

GARDEN PLANNING

Emmylou Harris once said in response to praise of her beautiful voice, "Our style is dictated by our limitations." Her limitations in range, power, and quality define her unique singing style—even if she wanted to, she couldn't sing any other way. As you plan your garden, be honest about your limitations and embrace them. Take a deep breath and ask yourself three questions: How much sunny space do I have in my yard? How many hours do I want to commit to the garden?

◀ **A little planning ensures you'll be happy with your harvest.**

And most importantly, what vegetables do I *want* to grow? From here, you can start building your (realistic) dream garden.

Decision Time

No single formula exists for a garden. It is infinitely customizable, which is exhilarating. But narrowing down the world that seed catalogs offer you can also be difficult. My main suggestion is to start with what you love to eat, instead of with what you feel like you should eat. There's no point in growing vegetables that you are going to struggle to use. What vegetables do you have a hard time finding fresh locally or in the quantity you want for canning or freezing? What are the vegetables you can't live without? I know I can't have a good season without a row of cayenne peppers and my favorite heirloom tomatoes. Think about what might be fun to grow; over the years I have tried lemon cucumbers, dinosaur kale, and all sorts of new things. Be sure to select varieties that thrive where you live. If your season is on the short side, consider choosing cherry tomatoes, for instance, instead of large beefsteak tomatoes, which would be more difficult to ripen to their optimal sweet and juicy level. Know your parameters, grow within them,

and experiment with simple methods for extending your season.

The key factors for choosing a garden location are sun (as much as possible) and accessibility (to your house and a water source). If this is your first garden, I suggest starting out small. It feels really good to be able to stay on top of planting, weeding, and harvesting, and once you get the hang of all these tasks, you can build on your experience. If your grand plan is to have four raised beds in your yard, perhaps start with one this year and see how it goes. I have seen many gardeners begin with one small plot, and a few years later the grass is but a memory. But having spatial limits can be a blessing too. I remember the overwhelming feeling of moving from the city to a suburban lot—I was stumped when faced with nearly half acre of garden design choices!

Succession Planning

My overriding goal for every season is a weekly harvest that is as diverse as possible. To accomplish this, I divide my planting into three rough categories: main-season crops, continual crops, and fast-growing succession crops. The main-season crops are those that structure and define the seasons, such as fava beans and peas in the spring, tomatoes and melons in the summer, and leeks and potatoes in the fall. Interspersed are crops that can be continually harvested from one main planting—such as basil, kale, parsley, and Swiss chard—along with fast-growing crops that you can plant in succession all season. Ideal plants for succession planting include beets, bok choy, carrots, frisée, kohlrabi, radicchio, radishes, salad greens, scallions, and turnips. Most crops you can harvest over several weeks. For example, you could plant a dozen

You may decide to buy corn at local markets because of the garden space it requires.

heads of lettuce and harvest three heads a week over four weeks. If that suits you, plan on putting in a dozen heads every month for the whole season. Planning those succession plantings will keep you stocked with your favorite vegetables for the entire season.

Another trick for having a diversity of crops every week is to plant larger successions than you could harvest all at once rather than thinking in terms of a single harvest. Take beets for example. If you go through the patch every week and harvest the largest beets this will give the remaining plants more room to grow and increase the amount of time you have fresh beets available. Like many vegetables, beets have no perfect size: you can harvest when they are the size of golf balls (chefs adore them) or as big as baseballs (more efficient for peeling and chopping).

Whether you have a large garden or just a few raised beds, I would start with main-season crops, and then fill in with continual crops and successions. If you don't end up with enough room for your spinach and arugula, grow one less tomato plant.

Crop Rotation

Crop rotation, alternating the location of your crops from year to year, is an important consideration with any style garden. Why? Some crops are very greedy when it comes to taking nutrients from the ground, and when annual crops are grown year after year in the same place the soil's nutrient balance is depleted. Moving your crops around also helps deter pests, alleviate disease build-up in the soil, and increase garden productivity.

The best way to rotate is somewhat debatable. Some experts suggest rotating crops based on plant family. This is because a disease that affects tomatoes, for example, also often affects other plants in the nightshade family, such as eggplants, potatoes, and peppers. The same holds true for other plant families such as brassicas (broccoli, kale, Brussels sprouts) and cucurbits (cucumbers, squash, melons). However, it may be difficult to accomplish this rotation method in a small garden because of the space required.

Another method that may be more practical in a small garden is to employ a soil-balancing rotation plan based on which nutrients crops most heavily use or give back. We can categorize garden plants within four basic types—leaves, fruits, roots, and legumes—which correspond to their feeding requirements. Leafy crops (such as kale and spinach) use nitrogen; fruiting crops (melons, tomatoes) use phosphorous; roots (beets, potatoes) use potassium; and legumes such as beans and peas are nitrogen-fixing

(meaning they actually give nitrogen back to the soil). If you are not going to plant peas and beans, consider just resting a portion of your garden annually to allow soil to rebuild. Consistent applications of compost, nature's probiotic, will also help keep the soil microbes in your garden balanced.

Below is a sample four-year rotation plan that you can use as a guide in your garden.

Garden Design

A garden can take many forms, depending on the space you have and how much gardening you want to do. Three basic setups are the "small farm," raised beds, and containers. Keep in mind that you can make changes to your garden from year to year, and you can always have some combination of the three structures.

SAMPLE CROP ROTATION PLAN

	Bed 1	Bed 2	Bed 3	Bed 4
Year 1	Leaves (use nitrogen)	Fruits (use phosphorus)	Roots (use potassium)	Legumes (add nitrogen)
Year 2	Fruits	Roots	Legumes	Leaves
Year 3	Roots	Legumes	Leaves	Fruits
Year 4	Legumes	Leaves	Fruits	Roots

THE SMALL FARM

This style of garden involves removing the grass from a section of your lawn and creating rows of plants, similar to rows of crops on a farm. The garden ends where the grass begins rather than utilizing a barrier. I am used to this type of garden, and it is typical where I am in the Midwest. It can be 10 × 20 feet or 50 × 100 feet, but it has the same feel.

Remove grass in such a way that it has no desire to return. The gas-powered method is to rent a sod cutter. Set it just below the surface of the soil and it will roll up your lawn like a blanket. Although you will lose the top inch or so of soil in the process, this will completely remove the grass. As a bonus, you can repurpose the rolled-up grass as sod in another part of your yard, or perhaps make a neighbor very happy. The other removal method is to smother the grass with heavy mulch or thick layers of paper and cardboard. You know how leaving something lying on your lawn makes the grass underneath turn yellow? Take that and magnify the effect with more layers. On top of the mulch, you can begin improving the

▲ Raised beds offer a number of advantages for vegetable gardeners.

existing soil by adding topsoil, sand, compost, and other amendments.

Once the grass is gone, you can use a landscape rake to define the beds, and then a steel rake to define the paths. After laying out the beds, you can start making decisions on the placement of the vegetables, along with any trellising, fencing, irrigation, or whatever else is needed, depending on your style and how long you think you might garden there. If you don't end up liking the location of your small farm garden, you can always convert it back to lawn and try another area.

RAISED BEDS

Raised beds help the soil warm more quickly in the spring, and in the case of heavy rain or flooding, allow the water to drain away from your crops. They are typically at least 8 inches high and rectangular. Avoid making them wider than 4 feet, otherwise it will be

Spinach and other greens are easily grown in containers.

difficult to easily reach into the center of the bed. In terms of complexity, raised beds run the gamut from mounded soil without a retaining wall to a more formal structure built from lumber, fieldstone, bricks, or even poured concrete.

Although you could always take them apart, raised beds are fairly permanent once constructed and filled with soil. Before you build the beds, carefully consider where to place them based on where the sun falls in your yard, and what materials you are going

to use. I suggest avoiding railroad ties and old painted wood so you don't add unnecessary toxins such as creosote or lead to your soil. If you aren't comfortable doing it yourself, hire someone to build your beds. You want them to last for a long time and be an attractive part of your garden design.

Do your research and find a trustworthy landscape supplier to provide soil to fill the beds. As raised bed gardening has become more popular, some supply companies have begun to offer specific soil mixes for this purpose, such as a combination of topsoil, compost, and sand. Experiment and amend as you see fit.

CONTAINERS

Most of us have likely done a little growing in containers, but if you have limited space or limited time, it might make sense for containers to be the whole garden. Containers can be a good way to begin gardening, giving you insight into how plants grow without committing your lawn to the enterprise. Growing in containers also allows you to be flexible and adapt to challenging gardening conditions such as a shady yard (or no yard at all) or poor soil. As with any vegetable gardening, container plants need as close to full sun as possible. But if it's your driveway or deck that gets the sun, you can place them there. When possible, try to locate plants somewhere visible because we tend to forget about things that we don't see regularly. Containers placed near where you enter your home, for example, will be easier to keep watered and maintained.

Container size is important. It must be large enough to hold an adequate amount of soil, otherwise the plant will consume the soil, fill the pot with roots, and become stunted. However, it must not hold so much soil that the plant is swimming in medium. As a point of reference, a tomato plant will need at least a 3-gallon pot, whereas a head of lettuce doesn't need much more than a half gallon. Those are the pot sizes that they will ultimately need, but I highly recommend starting your plants in small pots and transplanting them into larger pots once or twice as they grow. Choose a container with a drainage hole (or drill one) so it can shed excess moisture when necessary. Generally, containers need a lot more water than plants in the ground, so having easy access to a water source is helpful, too.

Use fresh, nutrient-rich potting soil to encourage steady growth. As far as soil goes, my favorite (albeit expensive) choice is a compost-based potting soil that is mixed with containers in mind and tested by a professional. It drains well, while still retaining moisture and nutrients. An economical option is to mix your own potting soil by following a recipe intended for containers. Container plants will also need fertilization of some sort. Use high-quality, organic fertilizer to ensure nutrients are slowly released for your plants. Skip the Miracle-Gro and other products that create lush, fast-growing plants, but leave your veggies less healthy and flavorful.

Planting Methods

After you have determined the layout of your garden, built beds, and amended the soil, you are ready to plant. Recommendations of how to sow are often listed on the seed packet. Here are some of the common planting methods, all of which yield different results.

- **Straight rows** are a traditional planting method for many crops. With a hoe, stick, or rake (and a taut string as a guide if you want perfectly straight rows), create the furrows, shallow trenches generally not more than 1 inch deep. Place seeds at the recommended spacing in the furrow and then gently backfill with soil. The seed packet will generally tell you how much room to leave between seeds and between rows. Straight rows do require leaving some areas unplanted (for paths to access the rows), which is a consideration if your garden space is very limited.

▼ **Make the most of your garden space by selecting the best planting method for your vegetables.**

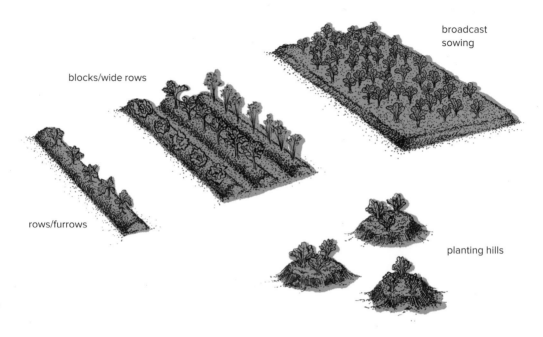

broadcast sowing

blocks/wide rows

rows/furrows

planting hills

■ **Blocks or wide rows** can help save space because you will need less room for paths. Just make sure that you don't make the blocks too big. You want to be able to reach in and easily harvest or weed your plants. Within the blocks, you can sow in rows, which is a good method for plants that you will be continually harvesting so they don't get too crowded. Or you can plant intensely within the blocks by broadcasting small seeds such as beets, carrots, lettuce, onions, and spinach. Simply smooth the planting bed, broadcast the seeds over the area, cover with a light sprinkling of soil, and gently water seeds in; you can thin plants later if they are growing too close together.

■ **Hills** are generally used for cucumbers, squash, melons, pumpkins, and other vining plants. Planting crops at the base of these small mounds of soil ensures excellent drainage and increased soil warmth, which is particularly helpful for these warm-season crops.

GARDEN JOURNALS

Keeping a gardening journal is an important gardening activity. I might think I will be able to remember everything that happened during the season and my ideas for next year, but that information often slips away over the winter. This record of successes and failures, weather, garden layout, and pests and disease will be invaluable. It will teach you more about your garden than any book could.

You can keep records in many forms. Consider starting your journal entry by recording the temperature and writing a brief statement about the weather. Organize your crop plan (what and how much you want to grow, your seed orders, and your planting schedule) in a spreadsheet with extra columns to write in what actually happened. You can also log harvesting and sales data in a composition book. Even if you're not selling your vegetables, it can be fun to keep track of what your garden produces. Not only does this give you some bragging rights ("I harvested 300 pounds of tomatoes this year!"), but when combined with weather and planting records, it can show if and perhaps why something went right or wrong.

As the season progresses, record garden layout (for crop rotation), fertilizer and amendments used, new varieties and planting methods tried, sources for seeds and supplies, pests and diseases identified and how you curbed them, flavor and quality of your produce, and perhaps any new garden-to-table recipes. Utilize a simple notebook or purchase a specially made gardening journal. Another idea is to save the informative plant tags from purchased plants and tape those into your journal.

Thanks to smartphones, it has also become increasingly simple to keep a photo journal. Take pictures at different times in the season to document plant health or figure out how much spacing between rows works best. Use photos to record seed packet information, or remember which areas of your yard are shady. Posting these garden photos on Facebook or Instagram creates a visual history of what you grew and harvested. Whatever you do, make sure you are keeping relevant records in a way that makes sense for you.

Get
Planting

A Focus: HOPE facility in Detroit provides local residents with fresh peppers and other vegetables and fruit.

JANUARY
Rest, Dream, and Plan

In Michigan the fall harvest is a distant memory by now, and the lush, warm, green spring is something we can only hope will come again. Rest assured, spring will arrive—and always sooner than we think. These are the days of hibernation and contemplation, and the time when seed catalogs start arriving in the mail. In January we are able to imagine a colorful and weed-free garden filled with amazing vegetables from seasons past and catalog pages. In this time of dreams I recommend dreaming big. Think Eden. We can put off the realities of tillage, sweat, and pests for a few more months.

◄ **Winter is the perfect time to plan your dream vegetable garden**

TO DO THIS MONTH

PLAN

- Start a new garden journal.

- Read seed catalogs (I particularly enjoy the writing in the Baker Creek catalog).

- Order seeds; choose varieties based on what succeeded last year, what you love to eat, and try some new varieties too.

- Go through leftover seed from last season and throw out allium, celery, and parsley.

- Germ test other seeds or use the seed life chart in this chapter as a guide.

- Draw a map of last year's garden (if you don't already have one) and plan crop rotation.

- Clean and organize seed-starting materials (including pots, lights, and soil) and order anything you are missing.

PREPARE AND MAINTAIN

- Prune fruit trees before they come out of dormancy—I like to wait for a relatively sunny, warm winter day.

- Check the quality of the vegetables in storage weekly; toss or use those that are starting to show slight rotting or mold.

- Check on any hoop house crops.

Zone 4   Zone 5   Zone 6

SOW AND PLANT

Everyone

- Start an indoor garden on a sunny windowsill with microgreens and kitchen herbs.

Zone 6

- Sow indoors (late in month): leeks, onions, and shallots.

HARVESTING NOW

From storage

- beets
- cabbage
- carrots
- garlic
- onions
- parsnips
- potatoes
- shallots
- turnips
- winter squash

HARVESTING NOW, cont.

From hoop house

- baby turnips
- beet greens
- frisée
- kale
- radicchio
- salad greens
- Swiss chard

Overwintered

- Brussels sprouts
- cabbage
- carrots
- leeks
- parsnips

Brussels sprouts seeds ready for planting.

Seed Ordering

Thumbing through seed catalogs on a cozy January night is fun and therapeutic. Although as an avid seed saver, my seed purchases are smaller each year, I keep the physical catalogs around because they contain a wealth of information, from conversion charts to seed spacing and germination temperature. I treat my catalogs as quick reference manuals, and as a result they are usually torn, tattered, and filthy by the end of the season. I wouldn't want my computer or my favorite gardening book out in the garden with me, exposed to the sun, rain, and wind, but my catalogs are expendable. If you are decluttering or simplifying, recycle the catalogs you know you will never use, but keep your favorites handy.

Start by making a seed wish list. Be prepared to trim it down later so you don't end up with significantly more plants than you have room to grow—or with crops that look stunning on the catalog page, but won't excite you when the time comes to eat them. Consider how often you want to have certain crops, which ones are your favorites, and the amount you need each time you cook with them, and lay out your garden accordingly. When ordering seed for succession crops, I recommend ordering a little extra so you don't run out mid-season. The seeds are small, and depending on how you direct seed, there can be a lot of variation in the number of seeds used per foot no matter how careful you are. However, if you do run out, most seed companies keep a full inventory of seeds all season long.

Before ordering, take an inventory of your leftover seed. Plant seeds deteriorate over time, especially if they weren't stored

HOW LONG TO KEEP SEEDS

1 YEAR	2 TO 3 YEARS	MORE THAN 3 YEARS
carrots	beans	cucumbers
celeriac	beets	melons
celery	broccoli	radishes
leeks	eggplant	spinach
onions	lettuce	
parsley	peas	
parsnips	peppers	
scallions	squash and pumpkins	
shallots	tomatoes	

properly (in a nutshell: cool, dark, and dry), so you can't assume that all of your saved seeds will be viable this year. The longer I grow vegetables the more ruthless I become with tossing out old seeds, especially if their germination rates have seriously diminished. The accompanying chart will give you a basic idea of how long to keep seeds, but I think it's smart to perform the seed viability test on all saved seeds before planting them again. Once you know what saved seeds are usable this season, you can go back and update your seed-ordering list.

Garden Mapping

A garden map will help you plan for rotations from one year to the next, and plan for succession planting within each season. Although you may think you will be able to remember where everything was, having a map is more foolproof. To begin, measure your garden plot with a tape measure. With your garden dimensions in hand, you can map your garden using graph paper (depending on the size of your garden, a square could be anything from 6 inches to 2 feet). Although your garden may not be a perfect square or rectangle, sometimes it is easier to illustrate it that way. Plan the spacing of paths, rows, and beds; add landmarks like your house and neighboring homes so that you know the orientation of your map. Note the location of trees or shrubs that will begin to shade your garden as the season progresses. For those who are tech savvy and inspired by accuracy, it can be fun to print an aerial map from Google and trace the outline of your property onto the graph paper. Be sure to photocopy your clean map before you fill in the vegetables. This can be your template for successions, and you can keep extra copies for the following season. Having extra copies allows you to make mistakes and play around with new ideas. You can also experiment with garden-planning templates and programs available on the Internet.

SEED VIABILITY TEST

The test to determine if seeds are still viable is simple.

▲ Make sure past-season seeds are still viable before planting.

STEPS:

1. Moisten a paper towel and line up ten seeds on it. Give them room to sprout by spacing them evenly.

2. Fold the paper towel and seal it in a clearly labeled plastic bag (record seed name and date of test). Set the bag in a warm place to germinate.

3. Look on the seed packet for the plant's estimated germination time. Once the expected number of days has passed for that particular seed, start checking to see how many seeds have germinated.

4. Count the number of seeds that germinated and multiply by 10 to get your percentage. So, for example, if only four (out of ten) seeds germinated, then the germination rate is 40 percent. The rule of thumb is to keep seeds that germinate at a rate of 70 percent or higher; if the germination rate is lower, consider tossing them. You can always try planting the seeds more thickly, but vigor tends to decrease along with the germination rate. If the seeds are special in some way, be sure to grow them out this season to replenish your supply with fresh stock!

Growing Microgreens

In a seed-starting station or on a south-facing windowsill, you can grow micro-greens from the seeds of arugula, beets, kale, lettuce, mustard, radish, spinach, Swiss chard, and many other leafy greens (look for pre-packaged seed mixes). Herbs such as basil, chives, and parsley will grow well too. Beside seeds, all you need for this fun and simple winter gardening activity is a shallow container with drainage holes; high-quality, compost-based potting soil; and water. As with all vegetable growing, the more light, the better.

STEPS:

1. **Prepare your container.** It's important that your container has drain holes because you want the soil to stay moist, but not wet. I use a commercial 10-by-20-inch open flat; another option is to recycle packaging you may have in your house, such as a clear plastic clamshell takeout container with several slits punched in the bottom for drainage. Fill your container with 1 to 2 inches of premoistened potting soil and smooth out the soil so it is evenly distributed.

2. **Sow seeds and provide water.** Take a pinch of seeds between your fingers and space the seeds about ⅛-inch apart in the prepared container. Sprinkle just enough soil over the seeds to barely cover them. Press the soil down lightly with a piece of cardboard cut to the size of the container to ensure good contact between the seeds and the soil. Mist the surface of the soil with a simple hand sprayer or a fogging nozzle. Avoid disturbing the seeds and soil you have so carefully arranged, but don't ever let the soil dry out.

3. **Wait, harvest, and start again.** You can start harvesting your microgreens as soon as the plants are a few inches tall (look for the emergence of the true leaves). Cut the microgreens just above soil level, rinse them off, and enjoy on pizzas, salads, sandwiches, or however you desire. Feel free to reuse the container; just fill with fresh soil and start the process over. The old soil makes a wonderful addition to your compost pile.

FEBRUARY
Tooling Up

Welcome to February: seed packages are arriving in the mail, the days are getting longer, and the forecasts include less snow. It is not quite time to get outside (except for shoveling and maybe a little pruning), but it is time for some indoor tasks. Work on organizing your seeds, both old and new, and get your seed-starting equipment ready to go. Check that your heat mats still warm up and your fluorescent lights still turn on: a little preparation can save a lot of time later. This month is still a bit early for most seeds, but if you want fall leeks and early onions, now is the time to start those alliums.

◄ From planning for spring to starting seedlings, there's lots to do inside while the ground outside is still frozen.

TO DO THIS MONTH

PLAN

- Order seeds, seed potatoes, and bare-root plants.

- Organize and order seed-starting supplies.

PREPARE AND MAINTAIN

- Organize, clean, and sharpen existing gardening tools; think about what you might need this year that you don't already have.

- Change the oil in your gas-powered tools and make sure they start; replace parts as needed or have them serviced.

- Complete pruning tasks.

SOW AND PLANT

Everyone

- Succession plant microgreens and herbs in your windowsill garden.

- Direct sow in a hoop house: baby turnips, beets, carrots, kale, salad greens, spinach, and Swiss chard.

Zones 5 and 6

- Start seeds indoors: celery, celeriac, leeks, onions, and shallots.

Zone 6

- Start seeds indoors: basil, broccoli, Brussels sprouts, cabbage, cauliflower, celery, celeriac, eggplant, fennel, kale, kohlrabi, leeks, lettuce, peppers, and tomatoes (toward end of month).

Zone 4   Zone 5   Zone 6

HARVESTING NOW

- Microgreens

From hoop house

- baby turnips
- beet greens
- frisée
- kale
- radicchio
- salad greens
- spinach
- Swiss chard

Overwintered

- carrots
- leeks

Get Your Ducks in a Row

February's peaceful, slower feel allows you the room to think big picture before the days start to slip through your fingers again. Take advantage of this month's downtime to get your tools in good working order and consider what additional tools might make gardening easier and more enjoyable. Perhaps something broke last year and you need to replace it, or maybe your repertoire has a glaring omission. I always have a long list of desired tools and I try to put them into the categories of "wants" (a tractor) and "needs" (two more hoes).

Certain core tools will be necessary no matter the size of your garden. It's best to stay away from bargain bins and dollar stores and purchase the best-quality tools that you can afford. Tools that you need daily or weekly should be pleasant to use and reliable for the long haul. But don't let having the "right" tools inhibit you from gardening. Acquiring new tools can be expensive, so approach it slowly and deliberately. You can always rent tools from local companies to test them before committing to the purchase. Rental companies can also fill in during those times when a tool is in the shop for service. Here are the tools that I consider essential in my garden:

- **Collinear hoe.** World-renowned gardener Elliot Coleman espouses the benefits of these hoes and I am right there with him. The collinear hoe allows you to stand up straight while you hoe. Its thin, sharp blade is designed to cut weeds off just below the soil surface, compared to a traditional hoe that requires bending over and moving lots of soil around.

- **Digging fork and pitchfork.** A digging fork is great for loosening garden soil or turning over compost; a pitchfork can't be beat for moving piles of mulch and spreading straw mulch.

- **Garden cart.** A wheelbarrow would suffice as well, but a cart with a larger capacity and flat bottom is a real convenience.

- **Landscaping rake.** A sturdy, metal garden rake makes quick work out of preparing beds. I like to have a wide, 36-inch rake to define the beds as well as a narrower rigid rake for the paths.

- **Leatherman multitool.** I use this tool for many purposes, from opening a box of seeds to tightening the screws holding my hoe blade in place.

▼ Having the right tools—and cleaning off the soil and debris before you put them away—makes gardening a pleasure. These are a few of my must-haves.

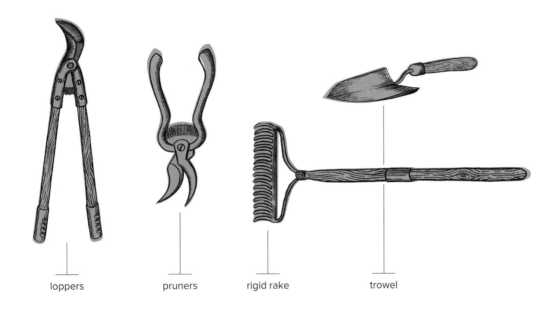

loppers   pruners   rigid rake   trowel

■ **Mallet (5-pound).** You'll want a mallet for tasks such as pounding stakes for tomatoes and peas or loosening rocks as you dig a hole; a large rock will also work in a pinch.

■ **Post driver.** This is an essential tool for pounding t-posts into the ground that can be used for fencing or constructing trellising for tomatoes, beans, or other vining crops.

■ **Pruners and loppers.** A good set of pruners is invaluable come harvest time. Loppers (basically pruners with extra-long handles) are a better choice when pruning large branches or harvesting Brussels sprout stalks.

■ **Spade and straight shovels.** I use these constantly for digging and edging. Heavy-duty is key; I can't tell you how many spade handles I've broken.

■ **Tape measure.** You'll need this primarily for laying out your garden, but it may also come in handy for corn-height bragging rights.

■ **Trowel.** A good stainless steel or aluminum trowel with a comfortable grip is essential for transplanting and hand weeding.

Your garden's size and style, and your budget, will influence whether you need additional tools. For example, owning a tiller can be quite useful if you have a larger garden, or you want to use it for weed control between growing beds and around edges. But if you only need a tiller once a year to prepare your entire garden, rent or borrow one. A broadfork is helpful for loosening the soil and incorporating soil amendments when preparing soil in the spring. You can accomplish a lot of the same tasks with a shovel or digging fork, so don't worry about the broadfork if you're on a budget.

Sharing Tools

A common observation among gardeners and small-scale farmers is that many necessary tools are used infrequently, often leading to the idea of sharing certain tools and maybe even creating a "tool library" for a neighborhood or group of gardeners. This may happen naturally in a tight-knit neighborhood if folks own tools such as a tiller, snow blower, or chainsaw. People who want to borrow the tool pitch in for gas and maintenance costs—or complete a simple exchange with a pie or a six-pack of beer. In lieu of informal arrangements, you could establish a more formalized, but still uncomplicated, neighborhood tool library; a Google document with a list of tools people are willing to loan along with the availability dates of those tools, would work. Beyond that, some cities—maybe yours—have larger tool libraries that are incredible community assets. Search online or contact your local extension agency or gardening nonprofit to learn more about location and membership.

Starting Seeds Indoors

Starting seeds indoors adds another layer of participation in gardening. It requires more effort, but it is immensely gratifying to grow the exact variety you want rather than whatever seedlings happen to be available for purchase. I have seen a wide range of seed-starting setups over the years, from quite simple to fairly elaborate. Along with a container and proper growing medium, you'll need sufficient warmth, light, and moisture or humidity to produce healthy seedlings that you can transplant into your garden.

▶ **Lights should be set around 3 to 5 inches above foliage. It is helpful to have an adjustable system so you can raise the lights as the plants grow.**

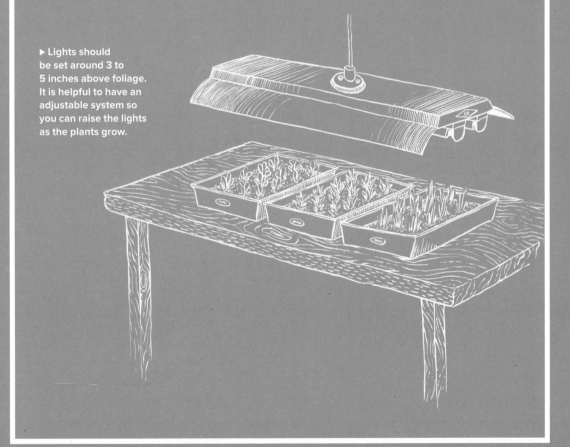

■ **Containers and growing medium.** You can germinate seeds in recycled egg cartons, peat pots, plastic flats (my favorite is the "288 flat"), and more. If you are plastic-averse, check out the soil-block system, in which lightly compressed growing medium serves as both container and soil. Johnny's sells a 20-block soil-block maker that creates ¾-inch square blocks (about the size of a 288-cell planting tray). The downside of starting seeds in small cells is that you will have to "pot-on" more quickly. For seed starting, I recommend a mix of peat moss and vermiculite. At this point, the seeds don't need any nutrients and you want a medium that will hold lots of moisture. Alternatively, consider using coconut coir to replace the peat moss as this is considered a more environmentally friendly medium.

■ **Heat.** Each type of vegetable seed has different ideal temperatures for germination; you can normally find this information (and much more) on the seed packet. For plants like tomatoes that need warm soil in order to germinate, I recommend the use of heat mats. They are available in various sizes and price points and are a worthwhile investment for growing any warm season crops from seed. You can purchase them at several online stores (see Resources).

■ **Light.** Unless you have a greenhouse or conservatory—and assuming your home is not made entirely of glass—you will need to supply artificial light to keep your precious seedlings from getting "leggy." Leggy plants are the opposite of stiff, strong, upright plants; they have grown too fast, producing a weak and long stem as they searched for light. Avoid this common problem by using an adjustable, full-spectrum fluorescent light. Position the light initially about 5 inches above the germinating seeds and adjust it as the plants begin to grow. The combination of the heat mats and the fluorescent light will create a professional seed-starting system that will pay for itself by producing sturdy plants.

■ **Moisture and humidity.** The goal is to keep seeds moist enough to germinate without overwatering—a common vegetable-growing mistake. Premoisten the potting soil and then apply all additional water with a hand mister. Sufficient humidity is just as (if not more) important to the germinating seeds. Lay a piece of plastic directly on top of the tray, or rig up some simple hoops with wire to keep the plastic raised above the soil.

STEPS:

1. Gather all materials and pre-moisten your growing medium so it is evenly moist but not dripping wet. You can do this directly in the bag, in a bowl, or on a tarp. If you are reusing any plastic containers, wash them in hot, soapy water.

2. Fill the containers with the moist seed-starting medium.

3. Plant your seeds. Use your finger (or a stick) to make holes in the soil and refer to the seed packets for guidance on depth and how many seeds to sow.

4. Cover seeds lightly with growing medium, press down gently, and mist with water.

5. Label each container with the name of the plant and the date of planting.

6. Place containers in a warm spot (on top of heat mats, if you have them) and cover with plastic sheets or plastic covers. At this point, the seeds don't need a light source. Check the soil daily and provide water if the soil is no longer moist.

7. As soon as the seeds sprout, remove the plastic covering and the heat mats (but keep the temperature above 60°F). Place containers about 5 inches underneath fluorescent lights for about 12 to 18 hours per day (an automatic timer is a smart idea). Water sparingly, allowing the soil to dry between waterings.

8. Following a seedling's first set of leaves, the true leaves will emerge (these look like the leaves of the mature plant). At this point any nutrients in your soil will be gone and it is a good idea to start feeding your seedlings with a small amount of diluted liquid fertilizer.

9. If a seedling is getting too large for its cell or container, and you still have some time left before transplanting outside, you will want to "pot-on," or transfer the seedling to a larger container with more soil (such as 3- to 4-inch plastic pots, 4-inch terra-cotta pots, or 2-inch soil blocks). Plants that are pale green or showing a bit of purple are stressed and definitely ready for a larger pot. You can also thin seedlings that appear crowded by snipping them off directly above the soil line.

10. Continue giving the seedlings light, water, and fertilizer until it's time to transplant.

Groundhog Remediation

Groundhog Day, February 2, is a good reminder to be on the lookout for damage caused by those cute, fuzzy herbivores with the appetites of cows. Few things are more irritating than transplanting some beautiful broccoli plants one day and waking up the next day to see little stems poking out of the ground. Groundhogs are especially hungry in the early spring as they come out of hibernation and begin raising a litter. If you have a problem, address it promptly; otherwise, groundhog mothers will soon be training their young on how to survive off your garden. If you are not interested in setting traps yourself, someone within shouting distance will probably love to help you out and show off their trapping prowess. You can also hire a pest control company.

■ **Havahart.** Found at most hardware stores, this old standby is a live trap, which means you will need to relocate trapped groundhogs to a large park or public natural area. These traps require a little patience and the right bait (cantaloupe is supposedly the best). Put the bait in the back of the trap, past the plate that trips the closing mechanism; you can also add a trail of bait leading toward the trap. Place the trap near the groundhog burrow if possible, or near the damage in your garden if you can't find the hole. Once set up, cover the trap with some leaves and sticks to help it blend into the environment.

■ **Conibear.** This effective method is not for the faint of heart, but if you are faced with a large population it might be the best solution. A few words of caution: these traps are indiscriminate, meaning any animal caught in them will be killed. Do not use if any small children or pets have access to your yard or garden: the risk is too high. It's unlikely that other wildlife will be caught in them because these traps must be set at the entrance to the groundhog burrow. Other animals would have to be unusually curious or trying to take over a groundhog's home. For groundhogs, you'll need a "202"-size conibear trap. This trap has incredibly strong springs;

I suggest you purchase the scissor-like tool usually also available for setting the trap. After the spring is closed, set the safety clasp that is attached to the trap right away. Catching your hand in these traps is as painful and frustrating as it sounds, so be careful.

Many people struggle with the idea of trapping groundhogs, but who are you growing food for—the groundhogs or yourself? Gardening will bring you face to face with all aspects of the natural world, some of which will overwhelm you with awe and beauty and others that will frustrate you and challenge you to make difficult decisions. As with all things in the realm of nature, trapping needs to be done with care, respect, and an understanding of our place in the world.

STEPS:

1. The first step is to locate the burrow. You may have to search a bit, but it is usually fairly easy to find a trail leading from your garden to the burrow.

2. Place the set trap at the entrance to the burrow, moving around some soil to smooth out the path if necessary.

3. Cover the area between the top of the trap and the top of the burrow entrance with sticks, but don't block the entrance.

4. A chain with a ring on the end is also attached to the trap. Pull the chain away from the trap, and pound a sturdy stake through the ring. You don't want the groundhog running away with your trap.

5. Check your trap a few times a day if possible to confirm that it is still properly positioned. Once you have a trapped animal, use that same scissor tool to open the trap, then remove and bury the carcass.

MARCH
Dig In and Move Out

March—when my greenhouse is filled with a vast sea of plants—is my calm before the storm. It is controllable and cozy, but I know that those plants are not going to stop growing, and soon I will need to transplant most of them. This will take effort and determination, and the calm organization of the greenhouse will be disrupted. I can imagine the neat rows of shallots and broccoli, vibrant green against the dark black soil, and seeing those rows will reward the long days of seeding in the greenhouse. March is a wonderful point in the season, and when July hits I long for these quieter moments and the cooler weather when anything seemed possible. This is not to say that March lacks activity. This is the time to begin preparing your garden: tilling, seeding, and setting up irrigation among other things. It is time to move out.

◄ Embrace the mud of March. Or at least use it to determine when your garden is ready for planting.

TO DO THIS MONTH

PLAN

- Update garden journal with spring weather and the challenges and successes of growing your own transplants.
- Finalize garden layout.

PREPARE AND MAINTAIN

- Turn compost if thawed.
- Incorporate finished compost into garden.
- Begin turning over soil and incorporating amendments as soon as weather permits.
- Test soil in vegetable garden.
- Erect fencing if needed to keep out rabbits and deer.

SOW AND PLANT

Everyone

- Pot-on transplants as needed after true leaves appear.

Zone 4

- Start seeds indoors: broccoli, Brussels sprouts, cabbage, cauliflower, celery, celeriac, kohlrabi, leeks, onions, and shallots.

Zone 4   Zone 5   Zone 6

Zones 5 and 6

- Start seeds indoors: basil, bok choy, broccoli, Brussels sprouts, cabbage, cauliflower, celery, celeriac, eggplant, fennel, kale, kohlrabi, lettuce, peppers, Swiss chard, and tomatoes.

- Direct sow (if soil is workable): beets and peas.

- Plant potatoes.

- Transplant (but be ready to cover): onions and shallots.

HARVESTING NOW

From hoop house

- baby turnips

- beet greens

- frisée

- kale

- radicchio

- salad greens

- spinach

- Swiss chard

Perennial and overwintered

- asparagus

- chives

- green garlic

- parsley (until it bolts)

- scallions

Turning Over New Ground

Now that the snow has most likely finished falling and the ground has thawed (probably still not true for those of you farther north) it is time to begin preparing the soil for planting. Any cover crops, leaves, and amendments have to be worked into the soil to make way for seeds and plants. The goal is a relatively smooth surface and consistency in the soil, although some chunks of soil and debris are fine. You can till by hand or with a rototiller, depending on the size of your garden. Turn the soil over at least a week before you begin planting to give it time to settle and begin absorbing the mixed-in materials. Within 1 or 2 weeks, weeds will arrive, eager to compete with your germinating seeds or transplants. Before you plant, gently rake the surface of your beds to kill off young weeds, but don't go too deep as that will just bring more weed seeds to the surface.

For hand tilling I recommend starting with a broadfork. Go deep and loosen up the soil but don't turn it over. After that use a spade or digging fork to gently incorporate cover crops, old mulch, and debris from last year. This can be slow and labor intensive so pace yourself and don't rush. If you are interested in making raised beds, this can be a good time to do that.

The goal of mechanical tilling is to loosen the soil as deeply as possible and mix it well at the same time. If you are breaking the ground for the first time in the spring, set the depth of the rototiller deep and go slowly. The tines don't need to be moving fast to do this thoroughly. If you need to go through again after you've already tilled once, set your tines closer to the surface to reduce the amount of weed seeds you bring up and lessen the risk of compaction. If you have permanent beds, don't worry about tilling the paths.

If you use a rototiller, avoid overworking the soil. Too much tilling at the same depth will eventually create what's called "hardpan" at the bottom of the tines. Plants can have a difficult time pushing roots through this compacted surface, and their growth can be inhibited. If you have that problem, use a broadfork to loosen the soil at that depth by pushing the forks all the way in and pulling back on the handles enough to open up the soil. Keep doing this until you have moved through the entire garden space. Too much mechanical tilling will also lead to loss of soil structure. When soil becomes pulverized, it compacts more easily, doesn't allow enough oxygen in, and can reduce the soil's ability to absorb and retain moisture.

▲ Planting tomato starts in the ground can be extremely rewarding.

Planting

The action of putting plants into the garden is rewarding. In just a moment a bare strip of soil is transformed into a garden. I tend to feel a strong affection for the plants I labored to produce in the greenhouse, and I am sure you will feel the same way. Putting them out into the garden is akin to sending your children off to college—it is time for them to leave your coddling and make it on their own. Here are a few ways to make this transition easier on the plants, and ensure they are equipped for the "real world."

Hardening off. The idea behind hardening off is to gradually expose your seedlings to full natural sun, cooler nighttime temperatures, and less frequent watering before you plant them in the garden. The sooner you can start moving your plants outside, the sooner they will become accustomed to the not-so-protected outdoors, and this will strengthen the plants. About a week or so before you plan to transplant your seedlings, set them outside for 1 or 2 hours of direct sunlight. Increase their exposure by about 1 or 2 hours every day and start to cut back a bit on their watering. The main issue that can come up if you don't harden off plants is the leaves becoming sunburned. This will show up as pale discoloration. The plants will recover

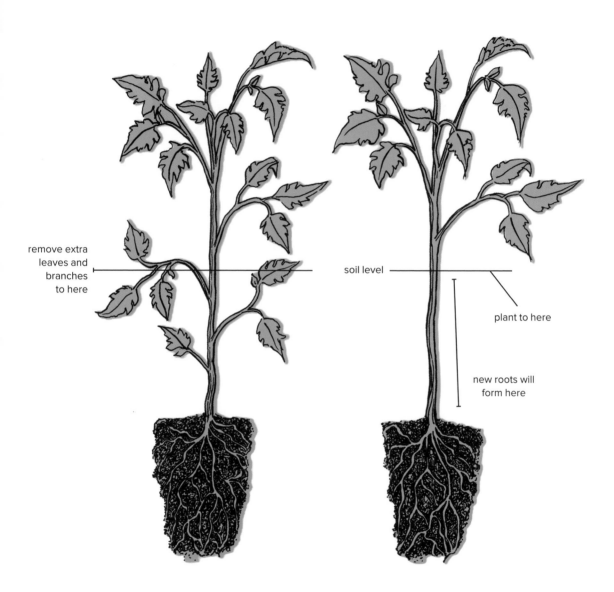

remove extra
leaves and
branches
to here

soil level

plant to here

new roots will
form here

▲ **Plant tomatoes as deep as their first set of leaves (remove
leaves before planting) to give them a well-rooted start.**

from being sunburned, but it will slow them down. If you are using good, compost-based potting soil, hardening off seems to be less of an issue, as the plants are used to growing in soil, which helps them through the transition. To help minimize the shock of the final transition, transplant on an overcast, windless day, or right before a light rain.

Soaking and fertilizing. I recommend soaking your plants in a tub of water (or any shallow container that can hold enough water to cover the pots) before transplanting. It can be advantageous to add a little fish and seaweed fertilizer to the water to provide nutrients and encourage the growth of beneficial bacteria around the roots. I also like to put some liquid amendments, specifically nitrogen, directly in the hole when I transplant. This gets the amendment right where the plant needs it

and avoids wastefully feeding weeds between your rows of vegetables. My method is to dig the hole, add the liquid fertilizer mix and let it soak in, place the plant, and then backfill the hole with soil.

Planting depth. The planting hole should generally be a few inches deeper and wider than the roots of the plant. Annual vegetable plants are not usually too finicky about depth, so don't overthink it, although certain plants will benefit from being planted deeper. For leeks and scallions, place plants halfway in the ground to achieve more of the preferable white part of the stem. Planting tomatoes deeply will give them a growing advantage because the plants will produce roots anywhere along the buried stem. Peppers should be planted similarly to tomatoes, although slightly less deep.

▼ If you have a particularly tall or leggy plant, dig a trench and lay the plant horizontally, turning the top up at the end of the trench. Be sure to remove any leaves that will be buried.

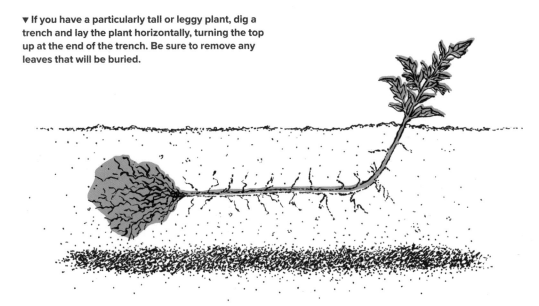

Mini Hoop House

This simple mini hoop house—a sheet of plastic secured over wire hoops—provides shelter for frost-sensitive crops in the spring and fall and protects plants from early-season pests. Note that this system is not sturdy enough to handle heavy snow and can be tricky to use when the ground is frozen. On days when the sun shines at all you will have to ventilate the plants by loosening one side of the plastic and folding it over; if it is windy, secure the loose plastic while it is open.

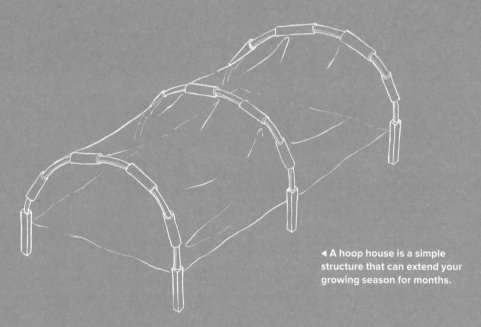

◄ A hoop house is a simple structure that can extend your growing season for months.

You can add a layer of Reemay (a lightweight polyester fabric) directly on top of the crops inside the hoop house to increase temperatures during the day and provide better frost protection at night. You can also use Reemay as a stand-alone row cover to protect against early-season pests.

YOU WILL NEED:

- 9-gauge wire for hoops
- 4- or 6-foot-wide plastic
- Garden staples, stakes, pegs, or bricks

STEPS:

1. Cut pieces of wire 2 feet longer than the width of your plastic. This will give you extra length to push the wire far enough into the ground for the hoops to remain sturdy. If your soil is really loose, you may want the wire to be even longer to get down into firmer ground. The number of hoops depends on how long you want your bed to be.

2. Set the ends of the wire 4 feet apart and push each end 12 inches into the ground to form the hoops. Space hoops every few feet.

3. Unroll the plastic along the length of your bed. If your beds are going to remain fairly consistent in size, cut the plastic to fit the bed, leaving a little extra to secure the ends. If the length of your beds might change, just roll up the extra and leave it on the end.

4. Pull the material taut and secure the ends of the plastic with garden staples or pegs, or drive in a sturdy stake and tie the plastic to the stake. Now go back and secure the sides. Fold the plastic over 6 inches so you have a double layer, which will keep it from tearing, and use stakes, pegs, staples, bricks, stones, or small bags of sand to hold down the plastic. Although it will make the hoop house less accessible, an even more secure method is to bury the edges (helpful in especially windy areas). You could also bury just one side and secure the other with a peg or staple.

APRIL
Nature's Seasonal Cues

Except in the northernmost areas of Michigan, everything is warming up. As plants begin to grow, ideas for dinner emerge and anticipation for summer harvests increases. April is similar to March in that a lot of preparations are still being made, but the difference is that most of it is happening in the garden. Seasonal cues continue to remind us of where we are. A flock of cedar waxwings reliably arrives every April and cleans up the remaining fruit on my American cranberry hedge. I imagine those raisined berries are a welcome treat as they get ready to pair off and raise their young. Similarly, we are cleaning out refrigerators and root cellars, using what is left of last year's productivity as we hope for fresh gifts from the garden.

◄ Plant a garden hospitable to ladybugs and other beneficial insects and they'll help keep your harvest pest free.

TO DO THIS MONTH

PLAN

- Keep up with your journal by recording how your transplants look, soil test results, weather patterns, and more.

- Purchase tomato, pepper, and eggplant seedlings if you didn't start them (or if yours didn't do well).

PREPARE AND MAINTAIN

- Pot up transplants as needed and begin hardening off.

- Continue preparing and amending garden beds.

- Design and build trellising for peas, tomatoes, and pole beans.

- Weed as needed and keep unused beds prepared by raking the surface.

- Thin transplants to recommended spacing.

SOW AND PLANT

Everyone

- Plant potatoes.

- Plant perennials: asparagus, berry bushes, fruit trees, rhubarb, and strawberries.

Zone 4

- Start seeds indoors: basil, broccoli, Brussels sprouts, cabbage, cauliflower, celery and celeriac, eggplants, fennel, kale, kohlrabi, lettuce, peppers, Swiss chard, and tomatoes.

- Direct sow: baby turnips, beets, carrots, fava beans, parsnips, peas, radishes, spinach, and salad greens.

- Transplant (but be ready to cover): broccoli, Brussels sprouts, cabbage, cauliflower, onions, scallions, and shallots.

Zone 4   Zone 5   Zone 6

Zones 5 and 6

- Start seeds indoors: summer squash and winter squash.

- Direct sow: arugula, beets, bok choy, carrots, kale, kohlrabi, lettuce, parsnips, peas, radishes, salad greens, scallions, shallots, spinach, Swiss chard, and turnips.

- Transplant: bok choy, broccoli, Brussels sprouts, cabbage, cauliflower, frisée, kale, kohlrabi, leeks, lettuce, onions, radicchio, shallots, and Swiss chard.

HARVESTING NOW

- arugula
- carrots
- chives
- lettuce
- parsley
- radishes
- spinach

be a balance between the insects we consider pests and those that provide significant benefits. The relationships between plants, animals, insects, and trees are complicated and mysterious, but we do know you can never have too much diversity.

As you plan, prepare, and work in your garden, consider the rest of your yard and the current landscaping. How could you attract more pollinators, beneficial insects, and insect-eating birds to your yard? Research what flowers, plants, and trees are native to your area, then narrow that list down to those that attract native birds and pollinators. A few Midwest favorites include butterfly weed, yellow coneflower, cow parsnip, American cranberry, New England aster, goldenrod, swamp milkweed, meadowsweet, elderberry, serviceberry, and red-osier dogwood.

Native plants usually take to their new home easily and grow quickly because that's where they want to be. They also often require less water and fertilizer than non-native plants and are less likely to be weedy. This can be a huge contrast to some of the fussy land-scaping plants that are readily available. You may be able to find some great native plants at traditional garden centers, but many natives will only be available through mail order—unless you are lucky enough to live near a native plant nursery.

Do it for Diversity

The emergence of ephemeral native plants and flowers is a seasonal cue marking the arrival of spring. The first of April is when wild leeks, or ramps, tend to be ready to harvest, and then around May 1 the trilliums on my farm usually bloom. Any variation on when they arrive tells me what sort of season we are having, either unusually warm or cold.

As I watch the forest come into its own, I consider what other native plants, trees, and shrubs I want on the farm. Creating biodiversity around the edges of the fields where the annual crops are grown has been a hobby of mine since I started farming. My philosophy is that a diverse edge habitat creates a healthier ecosystem, and the more likely there will

Supporting the Harvest to Come

In April peas are coming up and soon other crops will also be seeking support. This is a good time of year to plan out trellising and gather all the materials you will need. The goal of trellising and staking is to support

◄ Placing Midwest native plants such as swamp milkweed on the perimeter of your garden attracts pollinators, helps keep insect pests at bay, and makes the ecosystem of your plot healthier.

plants so they grow well and make harvesting easier. Growing plants vertically also conserves space and adds interest to the garden. If you have a small garden space, you might consider trellising crops that are not traditionally trellised. Cucumbers, for example, are well adapted to climbing and actually benefit from being raised off the ground. The fruits will be straighter and longer without the potential damage from having contact with the soil, and slug problems will be less likely because the plants will stay drier.

Some peas don't need any trellising and others will require significant support, but they all benefit from it. Shelling and snap pea vines range from 1½ to 3 feet tall, while snow peas can reach more than 5 feet. If you have one area in which you are growing different varieties of peas, it might make sense to plan on a 5-foot trellis for the whole row. Otherwise have a 3-foot trellis for the snap and shelling peas and a 5-foot trellis for snow peas. If you prefer shorter vines, you can choose dwarf varieties, which can be easier to manage and require less trellising. Pole beans have a similar growth habit to peas, but will require a taller trellis—7 feet if you can manage. Two ways to trellis peas and beans are the teepee method and in the row: let your garden layout be your guide.

▲ Three supportive options (from left): teepee, utility panel, or purchased decorative trellis.

TEEPEE

To make an easy garden teepee, set four stakes in a square shape, with about 2½ feet between each stake, and bind the stakes tightly at the top with wire or electrical ties. Any sturdy stake will do, but my favorite material is bamboo because it is attractive, flexible, and long lasting if brought inside during winter. If you have softer soil you can build the teepee and then position it in your garden. For harder soil it will be easier to pound in each stake at an angle and then bind the top together.

IN THE ROW

For this method, pound in the stakes deep enough until they are stiff, about every 5 to 6 feet. The distance is not critical, they just have to be close enough so that that the twine you string between them doesn't sag too much. Once the stakes are in, tie off your first piece of twine on one end, around 2 inches away from the ground. Pull the string taut to the next stake and wrap it around that stake at least once to keep it tight. You want it to be close enough to the emerging plants that they grab on right away. Place the next string around 4 inches above the first string and continue adding string until you get to the top of the stake.

◀ Garden teepees can help vine vegetables grow vertical and save room.

Steps to Bare-Root Planting Success

As the name suggests, bare-root plants are bare—they are dug in the fall after they have gone dormant and stored without any soil around their roots. Along with many native plants, perennial fruits and vegetables such as strawberries, raspberries, asparagus, and rhubarb are often sold bare root. The advantages to buying bare-root plants include lower price, better selection, and ability for plants to get established and grow faster. Bare-root plants do require immediate attention once they are in your possession, so study up on the steps to success.

STEPS:

1. Start with a healthy plant. Select plants that have healthy looking and established roots, and firm stems that aren't rotting or frayed. If you receive a mail-order plant that doesn't seem viable, call the company and request a replacement (always purchase from a reputable source).

2. Plant as soon as possible. Bare-root plants dry out quickly and if they are out of the ground too long, they will expire. It can be helpful to prepare the ground the preceding fall and have all holes dug and ready to go.

3. Soak the plant before transplanting. This process will wake up the plant and combat the drying-out process that has begun through shipping. Adding a little fish and seaweed emulsion to the soaking water helps encourage beneficial bacteria around the root system. Soak the plant for at least ½ hour up to 24 hours.

4. Dig a proper hole. Once you have decided on the location, dig a hole that is at least twice as deep and wide as the root system. An adequately sized hole gives the plant some loose soil to begin expanding into and gives you room to complete the planting process.

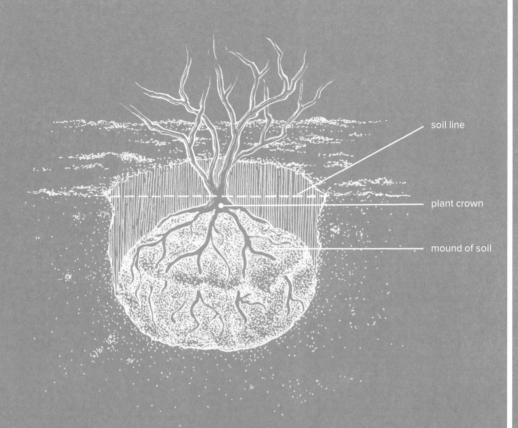

soil line

plant crown

mound of soil

5. Keep the crown at soil level. Mound the soil in the shape of a dome in the bottom of the hole at the depth of the root system. Then place the plant on top, spreading the roots around that dome. Next, cover the roots with soil from the hole, up to the base of the plant. You should be able to see a difference in the stem from where it was buried and where it was out of the soil. With fruit trees that have been grafted, you will see a sort of ring where the tree healed itself. Don't bury the plant beyond these points. Gently pack the soil around the plant to remove air pockets and stabilize the plant. If you are planting a tree or any large plant that might fall over in high-wind conditions, stake it for at least the first year.

▲ Place the crown of the plant at soil level and spread out the roots over the soil mound so that they will support the plant once the hole is filled.

MAY
Summer Is Almost Here

May marks the return to the farmers' market for many and the season begins with vegetable and herb plants, freshly cut perennial herbs, and overwintered crops like leeks. Spending time at the market, I get to hear a range of garden plans, from potted tomatoes on patios to nearly subsistence-size gardens. It is so rewarding to be a part of these gardening journeys, to hear about last year's successes and the goals for this season. During this same period, the birds, mammals, and insects quickly move from brooding their young to feasting on nature's abundance. We think we are growing our gardens for ourselves, but the rest of nature is pretty sure we are growing it for them! Get your defense strategies in line, continue growing or purchasing plants, keep weeding, pound in those stakes, and have your sunscreen handy: summer is almost here.

◄ There's a lot to do as summer approaches. Enlist some help and get your warm-weather seeds in the ground.

TO DO THIS MONTH

PLAN

▨ Make sure your kitchen is ready for the coming onslaught of vegetables, and start reading cookbooks in earnest.

▨ Keep up with your journal, adding information about pests and disease.

PREPARE AND MAINTAIN

▨ Continue to maintain transplants; thin out to recommended spacing.

▨ Remove row covers as needed so plants don't overheat under plastic.

▨ Look for signs of pests and disease and protect plants.

▨ Install and keep up with trellising.

▨ Weed, weed, weed.

▨ Ready your watering system. May can sometimes have dry spells that are detrimental to newly planted seeds.

▨ Zone 4 ▨ Zone 5 ▨ Zone 6

SOW AND PLANT

Zone 4

- Start seeds indoors (early in month): cucumbers, lettuce, melons, summer squash, tomatoes, and winter squash.

- Direct sow: arugula, beans, beets, bok choy, carrots, corn, cucumbers, kale, kohlrabi, lettuce, melons, peas, radishes, salad greens, spinach, Swiss chard, and turnips.

- Transplant: basil, bok choy, broccoli, Brussels sprouts, cabbage, cauliflower, celery and celeriac, frisée, kale, kohlrabi, leeks, lettuce, onions, radicchio, scallions, shallots, and Swiss chard.

Zones 5 and 6

- Be prepared to cover frost-sensitive crops in the event of an unseasonable frost.

- Direct sow: beans, corn, cucumbers, lettuce, melon, summer squash, and winter squash.

- Transplant: basil, celery and celeriac, eggplant, melons, peppers, summer squash, tomatoes, and winter squash.

HARVESTING NOW

- arugula
- chives
- fava beans
- kale
- lettuce
- parsley
- radishes
- rhubarb
- salad greens
- scallions
- spinach
- Swiss chard

to many problems, particularly mildew and other moisture-loving diseases.

Even with an observant holistic approach, you will experience outbreaks and emergencies. My general philosophy falls in the order of prevent, release, and spray. First, do everything you can to prevent an outbreak. If you have had issues in the past with certain pests, release beneficial insects. If all else fails and you are going to lose the crop, spray.

PREVENT

Methods of prevention include having a diverse ecosystem around your plants, keeping pots and trays clean, not bringing diseased or insect-infested plants into your garden, moderating water used to irrigate, amending your soil properly so it can feed the plants well, and planning enough space in the garden for good air movement. Covering young plants with Reemay will also help protect them from flea beetle damage. Flea beetles eat tiny holes in young tender vegetation; when there are enough holes, the plant can no longer photosynthesize, and expires. Row covers will also keep out cucumber beetles, potato beetles, and even aphids. A few tips for using Reemay:

- Cover plants as soon as they are planted or seeded; you don't want to trap pests in after they have arrived.

- Pull the edges and ends taut to prevent insects from getting in.

- For flowering crops that need pollination, remove the cover when flowers appear. At this point the plants should be mature and healthy enough to handle some insect pressure.

Dealing with Pests and Disease

As your garden begins to fill in and your vegetables start maturing, you will notice more evidence of pests and diseases. I hope that you will not encounter any major issues, but know that they are sometimes inevitable and out of your control. Although it can be tempting to fall into a "war on pests" mindset, a more holistic approach tends to produce better results. I try to refrain from going directly after the problem, and instead consider what circumstances allowed the problem to develop. A serious slug population, for example, points to an environment with too much moisture and not enough air movement, which is especially common in smaller, jam-packed gardens. In fact, excessive moisture and lack of air movement leads

▲ Attention to pests can make the difference between a thriving crop for you—and one that feeds the invaders.

You can use Reemay with or without the hoop system because the material is breathable and light enough to lay directly on top of plants. Just make sure you loosen it as the plants grow.

RELEASE

Not to delve too deeply into battle metaphors, but releasing insects feels like giving the losing army a mess of fresh new soldiers. Some beneficial insects to consider for your garden include *Aphidius colemani* parasitic wasps, ladybugs, lacewings, and praying mantis. *Aphidius colemani* parasitic wasps lay their eggs on the bodies of aphids. As the eggs mature into larvae, they eat the aphids from the inside out, leaving thin shells in their place. These wasps occur in nature, but not usually in large enough numbers to take care of an aphid outbreak, so bring in reinforcements. Lacewing larvae eat aphids, small

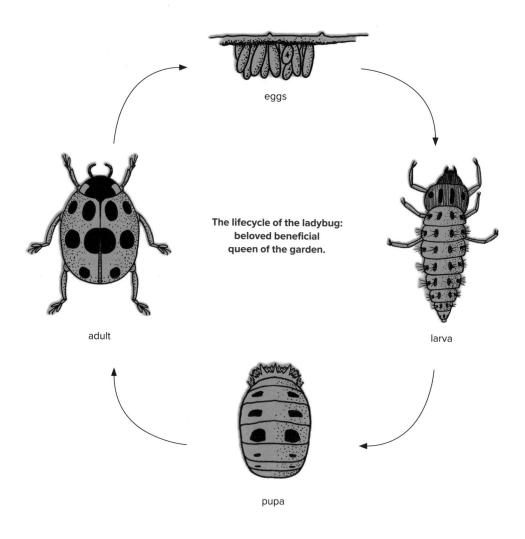

The lifecycle of the ladybug: beloved beneficial queen of the garden.

eggs

larva

pupa

adult

beetles, scale insects, leafhoppers, thrips, small flies, and mites; they will even eat each other, but I hope that is accidental. Ladybugs are also particularly useful in eradicating aphids, along with other soft-bodied insects like mites and white fly. The praying mantis plays a slightly different role because beyond being particularly fond of grasshoppers, it is not selective. It will eat everything in its way, including your beneficials. But if the pests are bad enough, praying mantis may help bring things back into balance.

SPRAY

If all the prevention and releasing fails, the final tool to combat a serious problem is spraying. In the world of organic growers even using the word "spray" is antithetical because of the strong association with spraying harmful chemicals and the perception that you failed in some way to prevent the outbreak. Although I recommend it only as a last measure, spraying can be an important part of the solution. As organic growing has gained in popularity and continues to evolve, more and more options are available. Always handle products with care, read the warnings, and follow all instructions. Also try not to spray right before it rains as most insecticides require ingestion and don't kill on contact. Some sprays that may work for you include the following.

Bacillus thuringiensis **(Bt).** This naturally occurring bacteria interrupts the digestive functioning of the insect. It is harmless to humans but kills the insect in a few days. It must be ingested, so apply thoroughly. Many gardeners have had great success with Bt on cabbage worm infestations.

Pyrethrin. This naturally occurring pesticide (derived from chrysanthemum plants) is toxic to many insects including aphids, earwigs, and thrip. Gardeners report mixed success with pyrethrin, but have found a newer version called PyGanic to be more effective.

Diatomaceous earth (DE). Made from ground-up fossilized shells, DE is extremely sharp on a microscopic level. To small, soft-bodied insects it feels like walking on knives, but to us it is as soft as flour to the touch. As insects move through DE they slowly dry out from the abrasions. To apply, put some in a cup and dust the plants; if possible, apply some on the underside of the leaves too, which is where a lot of pests reside.

Fungicides. Hydrogen peroxide and copper hydroxide will treat fungus, blight, and other bacteria—and both are acceptable for organic gardening. One challenge of fungal and bacterial diseases is that they spread through spores in the air, so make sure you apply weekly until you see results. Hydrogen peroxide is inexpensive and available from any drugstore. It is sold as a 3 percent solution; either use straight or dilute down as low as 1 percent. Copper hydroxide is commonly used on tomatoes to fight various blight problems as well as downy mildew, which shows up as a white film on the plants. Intersperse usage with hydrogen peroxide to reduce likelihood of the disease developing a resistance.

Fencing

Consider building a fence around your garden if deer, rabbits, and other four-legged furry pests are posing serious problems. Smaller pests, like rabbits and groundhogs, can't really jump or climb, so a 3- to 4-foot-tall fence should keep them out without impeding your garden access. However, to stop them from digging under you must bury 6 to 12 inches of the fencing material below the surface of the soil. Rolls of chicken wire and galvanized hardware cloth are fairly inexpensive and easy to use. Near where the fencing is sold you'll find metal stakes. Tie these to the fence for support.

If your problems are of a larger nature, you're not alone. Deer continue to move into heavily populated areas in greater numbers

and they've been a problem on my farm from the beginning. Fences around your garden need to be at least 8 feet tall in order to discourage deer from jumping over them. The good news is that the fence doesn't necessarily need to be expensive or permanent; even netting at the appropriate height will make a difference.

Using an electric fence system for deer, with flexible net fencing and a portable fence charger is an easy and effective system for managing deer predation. At the first sign of deer damage, you can quickly set up the fence in the critical area. For larger areas, consider using two wires instead of the flexible

▲ Don't wait to stop deer predation in your garden.

net, one about 18 inches high, and another 40 inches high, approximately the height of the chest of a deer. Pound in metal posts at the corners, and just enough posts along the sides to keep the wire from sagging. The idea is to make it relatively painless to set up and take down. Once the deer bump into the fence they will become wary. If they get shocked once they will not go near it. Even the wires alone may work because the deer will run into it, get confused, and stay away—at least for a while.

TIPS FROM THE FARMERS' MARKET

May is a good time to buy plants at your local farmers' market. It is a great way to get into the habit of going to market, and farmers can provide you with excellent growing tips. As you shop, ask a lot of questions about the particular varieties and how the plants were grown. Remember that all plants are not created equal. Many growers use tools and tricks to grow in a green-house that make the plants look good on display but will reduce your chances for success. Greenhouse-grown plants can be root-bound, overfertilized, or stressed from inconsistent water. You want to start with the best plants for your garden so inspect plants closely, purchase plants from a grower you trust, and be picky.

Weed Barriers in the Garden

Landscape cloth and landscape fabric. You can find these materials at hardware or home improvement stores and they usually come in a few different widths and lengths. Longer-lasting landscape cloth is made of woven strands of poly, which gives it lots of strength; landscape fabric is made from spunbonded polypropylene, which easily tears. Water easily gets through landscape fabric so you will likely need to replace it after a few years. To use either fabric or cloth, unroll the material along the length of your bed and lay out where you want your plants. Use scissors to cut 4-inch holes in the material (the holes should be big enough to trowel out the soil and plant). Since landscape cloth is woven, I recommend singeing the edges of the holes with a wand lighter to keep the cloth from unraveling. Secure the material with garden staples or bury the edges. Now you are ready to plant.

Agricultural plastic mulch. This material comes in different colors, widths, and lengths. The most common is 4-foot-wide black plastic. There are other colors of plastic mulch available—such as green (more warmth in the spring), red (for tomatoes), blue (for melons), white on black (for cool-weather crops; the white on top reflects the sunlight), and silver on black (to reduce aphids)—but

I am not sure how much difference they make. The basic black agricultural plastic mulch is intended for tomatoes and other crops that will appreciate the increased soil temperature created by the black plastic; it is not recommended for crops like broccoli and cabbage that prefer cooler temperatures.

Pick a day with low winds and unroll the plastic along the length of your bed. Dig a 4- to 5-inch trench the width of the plastic on both short ends and bury the edge of the plastic. On the sides, use a shovel and dig 4 to 5 inches down, just under the edge of the plastic. Take the soil you dug out and deposit it on top of the edge of the plastic. Slowly work your way down one side and then the other. You may have to kneel occasionally and pull the plastic tight as you deposit the soil. Next, place your plants, make holes for them with a trowel or scissors, and plant away. Using plastic in the garden is a matter of personal preference, although there are other, more natural alternatives to consider.

Organic materials. Straw mulch is easy to use and will contribute organic material to your soil as it breaks down. It tends to keep the soil cooler so use it on peas and other cool-weather crops (and for overwintering) rather than on heat-loving crops. Before spreading the straw mulch, make sure the

◄ Mulching helps conserve water and keep roots cool.

area is hoed and weed free, and wait until plants have matured a little so you don't accidently cover them. Starting with a 6-inch-deep layer will ensure that light doesn't get through and encourage weeds to germinate. After a few weeks this layer will compact down to 3 to 4 inches and create a nice mat. To avoid bringing problems into your garden, select straw that hasn't been sprayed with chemicals (residual herbicides will reduce the growth of nearby plants) and doesn't have too much grain or weeds left in it.

Wood chips, grass clippings, compost, bark, leaves, pine needles, sawdust, and grass are other possible organic materials—I have even seen a gardener use old church bulletins as paper mulch! Be creative and resourceful. Just make sure you don't bring in any unwanted chemicals. Also, if a lot of your organic mulch is "brown," use extra nitrogen fertilizer to make up for the loss that occurs as those materials break down. Wood chips, especially, absorb a lot of nitrogen until fully broken down. Composted chicken manure is an excellent high-nitrogen amendment.

JUNE
It's Growing Time!

Whatever the spring provided or denied you is in the past. The garden is in full force now and demanding your attention. You may still get some cool nights, but the sun is strong and the days are long. June is when gardens come alive and we start getting really excited for what's to come. We may be getting tired of the green garlic, spinach, and kale of spring and are ready to sink our teeth into the first ripe tomatoes of the season. In a perfect world, tomatoes should be available as soon as it is warm out. Of course, this is ridiculous, but the warm weather triggers all sorts of memories and desires. It is a short season in the north, and we want to wring everything we can out of it.

◄ **Fresh peas welcome summer in the garden.**

TO DO THIS MONTH

PLAN

- Plan for how to cook, preserve, and freeze your harvest.

PREPARE AND MAINTAIN

- Add string to trellises as needed.
- Keep up with weeds through hoeing and hand weeding.
- Look for signs of pests and disease
- Mulch peas, beans, and other crops.
- Hill potatoes.
- Irrigate as needed so garden gets at least 1 inch of water per week.

SOW AND PLANT

Everyone

- Continue succession planting: arugula, beets, bok choy, carrots, kale, lettuce, salad greens, and Swiss chard.

Zone 4

- Direct sow: beans, beets, carrots, corn, cucumbers, melons, radishes, summer squash, and winter squash.
- Transplant: basil, broccoli, Brussels sprouts, celery and celeriac, eggplant, kohlrabi, melons, peppers, summer squash, tomatoes, and winter squash.

Zones 5 and 6

- Direct sow (early in month): beans, corn, cucumbers, melons, summer squash, and winter squash.

Zone 4 Zone 5 Zone 6

HARVESTING NOW

- arugula
- beets
- bok choy
- broccoli
- cabbage
- chives
- cilantro
- fava beans
- frisée
- kale
- kohlrabi
- lettuce
- parsley
- peas
- radishes
- rhubarb

- salad greens
- scallions
- spinach
- spring turnips
- Swiss chard

A container garden of herbs and greens placed near your kitchen will make checking and harvesting easy.

Harvesting Guidelines

So many of the vegetables we grow will taste good and be useful at many growing stages. You can eat broccoli, for example, just after it sprouts, after it has grown to a 7-inch-wide head, and anytime in between. The trick is to harvest for what you want and to harvest when it is most efficient. Harvesting takes a lot of observation. Walk your garden every day and make note of the changes; the last thing you want is to miss an opportunity to eat what you are growing at its peak. It would take an entire book to describe each vegetable at its perfection, so I encourage you to keenly observe, feel, and taste your way through the process of harvesting. More details for specific plants are provided in the Edibles A to Z section, but it will help to get familiar with some general plant stages.

COLOR AND FIRMNESS

The key to observing color is to know what your varieties are supposed to look like when they are ripe. Catalog pictures aren't a perfect representation, but they can be really helpful. It also gets easier with experience, particularly when dealing with plants such as white or green heirloom tomato varieties (both will exhibit a bit of yellowing when they are ripe). Peppers are always a little confusing because any green pepper can be left on the plant to become a red pepper and orange peppers begin as green peppers. I mark rows or individual plants with labels, so I know which plants I plan to pick as green peppers and those I want to let ripen to other colors.

How firm or soft a vegetable is can tell you a lot about its maturity. A soft, loose head of cabbage or radicchio means it is not completely filled out yet and needs more time. However, if you grab a tomato to pull it off the vine and the skin gives way easily, you better eat that fruit immediately because it is nearly ready to be sauce.

FLAVOR

When crops are immature or past their prime, they lack the full flavor and sweetness that accompanies ripeness. My favorite way to tell if something is ripe is to taste my way through the garden. With most crops the method is simple: tear off a leaf, take a bite of a fruit, or dig up a root and chomp down. Does it taste good? Bon appétit. Just try to avoid the ones that are overripe—that might ruin the crop for you. Watermelon is the real boondoggle. Tasting your way through a watermelon patch will leave you with very few melons, so look for a curly tendril on the vine, next to where the melon is connected. If this tendril is brown and dying back, the melon is likely ready. After I've noticed the tendril, I do all the other stuff too, like sniffing and thumping, observing the color, and comparing it to what size I think it should be.

SIZE

The size at which you harvest is often a preference, but it points to maturity as well. When I harvest root vegetables, I look for ones that are "crowning," or coming out of the ground a little. It is not so much that crowning means they are ready, but more that I can see what size they are. If I can't see the root, I will gently run my finger alongside the row to feel the size. Overgrown beets, turnips, radishes, and carrots will eventually become tough, "woody," and often bitter.

CUT-AND-COME-AGAIN

This is the practice of harvesting parts of plants that you will let continue to grow. I generally let salad greens grow to around 5 inches and cut the top half, leaving the bottom half of the plant to regrow. If you cut too low, you risk cutting the part of the plant from which new growth will come. I can usually get around three cuttings (one per week) before the plants become a little ragged. For crops like kale, parsley, and Swiss chard, another method is to simply pick off outer leaves, starting from the bottom, and let the heart of the plant keep producing. This keeps the plants cleaned up and tidy, too.

BOLTING AND SPLITTING

Bolting is when a vegetable flowers when you don't want it to and the flavor profile changes. The goal of any plant is to propagate by producing seeds, which starts with a flower. Fruiting crops, like zucchini and eggplants, flower first and what you want are the seeds surrounded by their delicious fruit. However, with vegetables such as arugula and lettuce, we want the leafy part rather than the seed. Bolting is to be avoided, but it's not always the end of the world. A bolted plant is simply an opportunity to practice your seed saving skills.

Cabbage, cherry tomatoes, kohlrabi, and radishes commonly split when they are past their prime. This can also happen if a plant gets a lot of water right after a dry spell. They have a huge growth spurt and their skins can't keep up. When you start to see plants splitting, know that nearby ones will probably split soon as well, so it is time to harvest.

Trellising Tomatoes

The most common way to trellis tomatoes in a garden is with a tomato cage. Cages are easy to set up and provide a decent amount of support. Use a larger cage for indeterminate varieties that continue to grow and produce throughout the season, and a smaller size for determinate tomatoes which grow to a fixed mature size and ripen all of their fruit in a relatively short period. For additional support, which is particularly useful in preventing wind damage, pound a stake alongside the cage and fasten the stake to the cage with twine.

▶ **Cages are a simple and quick way to support tomatoes.**

▲ Support a row of tomatoes with just string and stakes using the Florida weave technique.

The Florida weave, named after the tomato-growing capital of the United States, is another effective technique to support tomatoes. All you need are 6-foot stakes, a roll of twine, and scissors. To begin, plant your tomatoes 2 feet apart in a straight row and drive a stake between every plant. When the tomatoes look like they need support, usually when they are around 12 inches tall, you can start stringing the plants.

Start by tying the twine to the first stake (at the equivalent of about halfway up the plant). Pull it taut and loop it around the rest of the stakes in the row. Make a double loop around the last stake and repeat the process at the same height on the other side of the tomatoes. When you return to the first stake, make a tight knot and cut off the twine. Add subsequent strings weekly, about every 4 to 8 inches, until plant growth stops.

JULY
Hot and Bothered in the Garden

July always seems to creep up on me. Time speeds up because there just isn't enough of it. The sweet, cool, calm, early season has transitioned into being hot and bothered—a little like coming of age. As tractors break down, pests multiply, weeds grow, and time becomes my master, I ask myself: Is this what I was looking forward to? But it starts to make sense as I fall in love: crisp cucumbers, the first dead-ripe tomato, and eating whole peppers like apples. The joy of becoming buried in vegetables makes up for the complexity, just as the teen years open up a world of emotions and ideas you never knew existed.

◄ July is a month of plenty—enjoy the bounty, including fresh greens from the garden.

TO DO THIS MONTH

PLAN

- Start planning your fall garden.
- Record harvesting results in your garden journal.
- Order garlic for fall planting.

PREPARE AND MAINTAIN

- Hill potatoes.
- Add string to trellises as needed.
- Keep up with weeds through hoeing and hand weeding.
- Remove spring crops like peas that are finished producing.
- Irrigate as needed so garden gets at least 1 inch of water per week.
- Turn compost and make sure it stays moist enough.

SOW AND PLANT

Everyone

- Sow indoors for fall garden: broccoli, Brussels sprouts, cabbage, cauliflower, kale, and Swiss chard.
- Continue succession planting: arugula, basil, beets, bok choy, kale, and Swiss chard.

Zone 4

- Direct sow: beans, beets, carrots, kale, lettuce, radishes, and turnips.

Zones 5 and 6

- Make final succession plantings of bush beans.

Zone 4   Zone 5   Zone 6

HARVESTING NOW

- basil
- beans
- beets
- bok choy
- broccoli
- cabbage
- carrots
- chives
- cilantro
- cucumbers
- eggplant
- garlic
- frisée
- kale
- kohlrabi

- lettuce
- melons
- onions
- parsley
- peas
- peppers
- potatoes
- radishes
- radicchio
- salad greens
- scallions
- summer squash
- Swiss chard
- tomatoes
- zucchini

you can easily move the plants around to find the perfectly cool spot as they germinate. It will also be easier to keep the soil moist because you can keep the plants near your house—and the spigot.

When trying to grow cool-season crops in July, remember that water creates an efficient cooling system through evaporation. The heat can be overwhelming in the greenhouses in the summer, but if I soak the floor, the temperature drops 10°F. This same effect happens on the ground. Don't overwater; just make sure during germination that the soil stays moist, so the "cooling system" is always on.

Harvesting in the Heat

When harvesting begins in earnest, keeping up with production and finding a home for all your vegetables are good problems to have. But it is important to handle your vegetables well so they stay fresh for you and any benefiting friends and neighbors. Here are some general guidelines for keeping produce fresh, even if it is only stored for a short period of time.

Harvest at the right time. I find it difficult to work effectively when the temperatures peak in the late afternoon, and I think plants feel the same way. Who likes to be yanked around when you are already hot and cranky? I like to harvest most leafy vegetables in the morning with dew still on them and before they wilt from the sun. It's okay if plants wilt, a natural defense against heat, but avoid harvesting during that time. Harvesting when plants are wilting and under stress can add

Beat the Heat

The heat of July brings fruits into production, but it can also wreak havoc on crops that prefer cool weather. When this happens, you can let go and wait for the weather to become favorable for those crops again, or find ways to cope. For crops that refuse to germinate when it is too hot (spinach and lettuce, for example, prefer temperatures below 75°F), look for a growing area with some shade or try intercropping in your current garden space. Tomatoes, pole beans, corn, and other tall crops can provide enough shade to keep the soil cool, but still let in enough sun to allow for good growth. Intercropping works well when the main crops need space to grow, but in the meantime bare soil is available. Timing is critical.

Another way to sidestep the heat is to start leafy greens in pots or flats and transplant them. The advantage of this method is that

Inconsistent watering can result in cracked tomatoes. They are fine to eat , but do so as soon as possible.

some bitterness to their flavor, especially to the leafy crops. It also makes it harder to cool them down after they are picked, which shortens their shelf life. Harvest fruits midday when possible because the plants will be dry, which reduces the spread of disease. For a few crops, especially basil and salad greens, harvesting during the evening is best. They seem to be more robust as they regain strength after enduring the heat.

Trim and top root crops. For root crops that have tops, like radishes and beets, take the tops off immediately. They continue to respire once they are out of the ground and the roots will quickly become rubbery if the leaves are left on. If you are going to eat the tops, store them separately.

Cool vegetables down quickly. Plants hold their heat from the garden for a long time. The best way to get that "field heat" out of

them is to fill up your kitchen sink with cold water and let them soak for ten minutes right after harvesting; this is known as hydrocooling. The water temperature will rise quickly as it absorbs the heat from your vegetables. Some herbs, as well as beans and peas, are better stored dry or they will mold quickly. Basil can actually quickly turn black if washed and stored wet. Instead, these items should be washed immediately before using.

Dry thoroughly before storing. Water is great for cooling and washing, but not for storing. After washing salad greens, toss them in a salad spinner to dry. You can shake tougher greens like beet greens, kale, and Swiss chard or pat them dry with a towel. Store greens in a closed container or bag to keep them from losing all their moisture. Until they are consumed, vegetables are living food, and proper storage is akin to life support.

Intercropping with Cover Crops

Intercropping is a great way to provide leafy greens with shade, but you can also use this method to improve your soil and suppress weeds by planting a cover crop. The best cover crop for intercropping is a mixture of annual rye grass and Dutch white clover (a dwarf clover). The grass provides a thorough weed barrier while holding the soil in place and building soil structure. Also, this is an annual grass that dies back in winter, so it won't form an undesirable sod in the garden. Clover does those things too, along with adding nitrogen to the soil. However, clover isn't as good at quickly covering the soil as annual rye grass, so the mixture works best.

▶ **A good way to take advantage of the shady space near tomatoes is to intercrop with broccoli, which loves cool temperatures.**

▲ Clover is a great cover crop, adding nitrogen to soil.

STEPS:

1. Transplant or seed your main crop and allow it to begin to mature. Give the vegetable crop time to become established before planting the cover crop so that it doesn't compete too much.

2. Weed the area between rows that you want to plant in. Use a rake and smooth out the soil.

3. Broadcast the cover crop mixture of annual rye grass and Dutch white clover. Lightly rake the seed into the soil, disturbing only the top inch or two.

4. Water immediately after planting and then once a week (or as needed, depending on rain) until the intercrop is established.

AUGUST
The Dog Days of Summer

The heat of July continues into August with no end in sight. In these dog days of summer, lying around in the shade and cooling off in the nearest body of water are the most appealing activities—and jobs in climate-controlled cubicles begin to sound better and better! On the positive side, weeds die quickly after they are hoed or pulled out in the hot weather, compared to when they seem immortal in April and May. The other obvious bright spot in this labor and heat is the sheer beauty and abundance of the harvest. All the different crops—from yellow squash and purple eggplants to multicolored cherry tomatoes—make the gallons of sweat and water worth it.

◀ **If your August garden gives you more than you can eat, pickling, drying, and canning can prevent waste and preserve the taste of summer for colder months.**

TO DO THIS MONTH

PLAN

- Add temperature data and harvest quantities to journal.
- Lay out the fall and winter garden spaces on paper.
- Order garlic for fall planting.

PREPARE AND MAINTAIN

- Add string to trellises as needed.
- Keep up with weeds through hoeing and hand weeding.
- Stay on top of irrigation.
- Keep your kitchen organized and ready to cook and preserve.
- Side-dress plants with compost.

SOW AND PLANT

Everyone

- Sow cover crops.
- Continue succession planting: bok choy, fall radishes, and salad greens.
- Transplant: broccoli, Brussels sprouts, cabbage, cauliflower, kale, and Swiss chard.

Zone 4

- Plant garlic in the middle to end of the month.

Zone 4   Zone 5   Zone 6

HARVESTING NOW

- basil
- beets
- bok choy
- broccoli
- carrots
- chives
- cucumbers
- eggplant
- frisée
- kale
- kohlrabi
- melons
- parsley
- peppers
- potatoes
- radicchio
- radishes

- salad greens
- scallions
- summer squash
- Swiss chard
- tomatoes
- zucchini

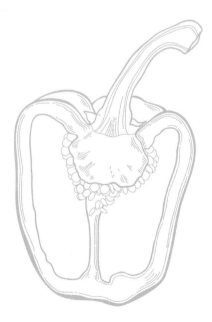

Thinking Ahead

It's easy to get distracted with harvesting, but August is the time to direct seed crops for the fall. Best bets are crops such as beets, turnips, and storage radishes; avoid heat-loving crops like squash, peppers, and tomatoes because the weather will become too cold at this point to push the plants to produce fruit. The August garden can be inhospitable for newly planted seeds so keep plants watered during germination and maintain a well-groomed and weed-free bed. The goal is to pamper those new seedlings to help them thrive.

When planting in the spring you have some wiggle room, because the entire season is still ahead of you, but timing is everything with fall planting because a strict deadline awaits: frost. As you plan, keep in mind that as the season progresses, daylight and temperatures decrease, so it will take longer for plants to

▲ **Green beans are a good choice for seed saving.**

mature. A good rule of thumb is to add 2 weeks to the days-to-maturity figures listed on the seed packet. Red Ace beets, for example, typically mature in 50 days, so give them 64 days in your fall planting plan. In other words, if you want them to be ready on October 1, plant on July 27.

Here are some ideas for your fall planning purposes of how long plants take to mature. But remember that even though certain crops, such as kale, may take 60 days to reach their fully mature size, they will still be delicious when harvested in half that time as baby greens.

PLANT MATURITY

PLANTS THAT MATURE IN 3 MONTHS	PLANTS THAT MATURE IN 2 MONTHS	PLANTS THAT MATURE IN 1 MONTH OR LESS
Brussels sprouts	beans	baby turnips
cabbage	beets	*basil
cauliflower	carrots	bok choy
fall leeks	chard	cilantro
*potatoes	*cucumbers	frisée
	*dill	kohlrabi
	fennel	lettuce
	kale	radishes
	radicchio	scallions
	turnips	spinach
	winter storage radishes	

*Plants killed by frost

SHARING AND SAVING THE HARVEST

In August the garden is in full production with a complete range of vegetables coming in and the fixings for gorgeous, fresh meals at your fingertips. But many gardeners find that this bounty can sometimes become overwhelming without friends, family, officemates, and neighbors who are eager to benefit from your overflow. Not only does sharing lighten your load, it can also provide connection points to fellow gardeners and community members. Research Plant a Row for the Hungry, or other organizations that offer ways to donate your produce. Inherently communal, food is something around which to come together.

This is also the time to "put up" different fruits and vegetables in earnest: in the middle of winter, you'll be so happy you did. My grandmother loved to can tomatoes, my wife enjoys making kimchi, and another friend loves plain old tomato juice for her husband's health regimen. My suggestion is to begin with what you know you love and branch out from there. Experiment with dehydrating, pickling, and freezing, too. Your local extension service is often a great resource for learning safe and fun ways to preserve your harvest.

Side-Dressing

By August, many plants that have been continuously setting fruit all season will need some extra nutrients. Side-dressing is a fancy word for late-season fertilizing right in the row. A great way to boost nutrients and simultaneously amend the soil is by side-dressing with both fertilizer and compost. Making your own side-dressing is pretty easy. All you need is a wheelbarrow, a shovel, mature compost, and an all-purpose, organic vegetable fertilizer. Look at the fertilizer directions to figure out how much fertilizer to use and to decide approximately how thickly you want to apply the compost.

Say you want to put a shovelful of compost by each tomato plant and the fertilizer directions say to use a ½ cup of fertilizer per plant. For every shovel of compost in the wheelbarrow, toss in a ½ cup of fertilizer, and mix thoroughly. Using that same shovel, carefully spread the mix around your plants, working it gently into the soil so that it reaches the roots more effectively. The Michigan-based company Dairy Doo makes an excellent product which contains compost and an array of necessary nutrients for plant development, which I highly recommend if you don't want to make your own mixture.

▶ **With fertilizer and compost, side-dress annual vegetables, perennial edibles, and any other landscaping that needs a nutritional boost.**

Save Your Garlic Seed

Garlic seed is rather expensive, but after you buy it once, you can save your own seed indefinitely. In my experience, the saved garlic just gets better and better as it adapts to your soil. And when you save your own, you can also select for the qualities you like best. I prefer big bulbs with five or six cloves, for example, so I put those aside and use the smaller bulbs with too many or too few cloves for my liking.

Some tips for saving garlic seed:

■ As you harvest your first season of garlic, save cloves from the garlic plants with your favorite qualities, such as their size or number of cloves.

■ Don't peel the garlic. Gently break apart the bulbs, but leave the outer skin on so that they are protected.

■ Keep cloves you are saving for seed in the same cool, dry place you will store the rest of your garlic.

■ Don't worry if your saved cloves start sprouting a little. Garlic planting (September or October, depending on where you live) is just around the corner from harvesting (usually July), so they won't have to sit in storage for too long.

SEPTEMBER
A Bountiful Harvest Awaits

September is a continuation and sometimes acceleration of August's harvesting bonanza as some fall crops (like celery, winter squash, and leeks) begin to show up, while summer crops are still in peak. This month of transition holds both summer and fall within its days. You still have roughly a month of decent growing weather, but plants now grow at about half their normal rate. As tempting as it might be to squeeze in another succession, it is probably too late to direct seed crops outside, unless you live in zone 6. If you are using a greenhouse, row covers, or another form of protection, you can extend the season past September.

◄ **Kids love seeing their garden edibles ripen for harvest.**

TO DO THIS MONTH

PLAN

- Record temperature data and harvest quantities in garden journal.

- Get season-extension tools in place and ready to go.

- Check indoor growing supplies (seeds, potting soil, and containers) and make sure that your lights turn on.

PREPARE AND MAINTAIN

- Acquire mulch.

- Clean and prep storage room.

SOW AND PLANT

Everyone

- Sow cover crops.

Zones 5 and 6

- Plant garlic in the middle to end of month.

Zone 6

- Direct sow: arugula, beets, broccoli, carrots, frisée, kale, lettuce, radishes, salad greens, and spinach.

Zone 4   Zone 5   Zone 6

HARVESTING NOW

- bok choy
- broccoli
- carrots
- chives
- cucumbers
- eggplant
- frisée
- kale
- kohlrabi
- lettuce
- melons
- parsley

- peppers
- potatoes
- radicchio
- radishes
- salad greens
- scallions
- summer squash
- Swiss chard
- tomatoes
- winter squash
- zucchini

If you still have crops in the ground, you can intercrop your cover crops. This works better with fall crops like Brussels sprouts and broccoli than with vines and shrubby crops like tomatoes. I don't recommend intercropping cover crops with salad greens as it will interfere too much with harvesting and you may end up with a lot of rye sprouts in your salad.

Another way to put your garden to rest is with mulch. Mulch protects the soil from freezing and thawing. It will break down over the winter into a nice soil amendment, and for some early spring crops it can be pushed aside for planting and continue to provide some warmth and weed control for spring growth. Materials that can be used include fall leaves, straw, leaf mold, and grass clippings.

Preparing the Garden for Rest

September is the time to prepare your garden for the winter. One practice to consider is fall cover cropping. The fall is a nice time to plant cover crops because the soil tends to be moist, and the temperatures are more amenable for germination. Cover cropping can help build the structure of your soil while adding organic matter and potentially nitrogen. In September you still have time to plant annual rye grass and clover, the same mix I recommend for intercropping. Other options include winter wheat, barley, and rye. I have leaned heavily on fast-growing hardy rye because you can plant it in late September and it will continue to establish itself even as nights drop below freezing.

Storing the Harvest

September is also a good time to make sure you are ready to store vegetables such as turnips, carrots, potatoes, parsnips, winter squash, beets, cabbage, and onions for the winter. Every crop has ideal storage conditions, but cool, dark, and dry are generally the most important. If you can find or create a space that is around 50°F with low humidity, you should do well. An unfinished and unheated basement in an older house is a good option. Garages can work until temperatures start hitting the freezing point, although a consistent temperature is preferred even if it is slightly on the warmer side.

Refrigeration will provide the consistent, lower temperatures that keep vegetables in dormancy for a long time. It also has the benefit of keeping out light. The only concern with refrigeration, besides cost, is that it

MAKING LEAF MOLD

What is leaf mold? It couldn't be simpler—it's just the rich, crumbly, earthy-smelling compost created when leaves decompose. Yes, all those leaves falling from your tree right now. This spectacular, and spectacularly free, soil amendment will drastically increase water retention, improve soil structure, and encourage soil life. It takes about a year to create leaf mold, but very little of that time requires any effort on your part. Start by gathering your leaves into a big open pile, bin, or plastic bag (poke holes in the bag for air flow) in an out-of-the-way part of your yard. Water the leaves to dampen and continue to monitor periodically so it remains moist. You can speed decomposition by shredding the leaves (run over them a few times with a lawn mower) before piling or bagging them; you can also turn over your pile with a shovel or shake your bag every couple of weeks.

continuously removes moisture. If refrigerating root vegetables, I recommend placing them in perforated plastic bags. This makes a huge difference in retaining moisture. I have had bags of beets harvested in September store through April; without the bag the beets would shrivel like shrunken heads.

If you don't have a workable basement or refrigeration setup, consider creating a simple DIY root cellar with a 5-gallon plastic bucket (or multiple buckets if you need more space) buried in the ground. You'll need to dig a hole deep enough to fit all but the top few inches of the bucket. Put your storage vegetables inside and cover with a tight-fitting lid. Place a tarp over the bucket to keep moisture out and hold the tarp down with a brick or other heavy object. If you live in an area with particularly cold winters, it's smart to add a thick layer of mulch or straw on top of the lid (underneath the tarp) for extra insulation. Be sure to mark the area clearly so you don't trip on the bucket or forget where it is when it snows!

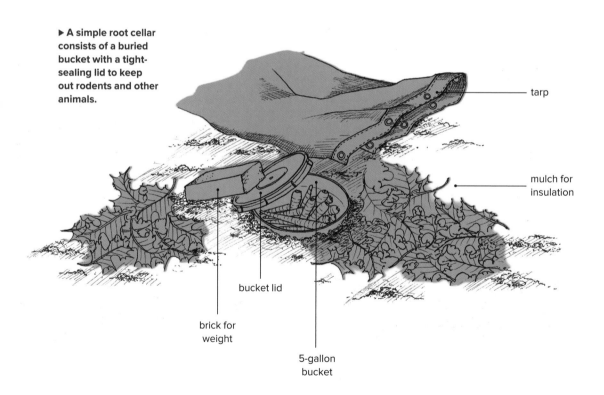

▶ A simple root cellar consists of a buried bucket with a tight-sealing lid to keep out rodents and other animals.

tarp

mulch for insulation

bucket lid

brick for weight

5-gallon bucket

Last-Chance Frost Protection

When you desperately want to save a crop for a few more harvests, but you know it is going to freeze for a night or two, try a somewhat counterintuitive protection method: irrigation. Don't worry if a layer of ice forms around the plant in extreme cases. The warmth from the living plants will be trapped in that "igloo" and protect it from freezing. The plant may appear damaged or yellow, but it will be alive and should easily bounce back.

STEPS:

1. Choose a sprinkler that can produce a low-volume mist. Rotary-type sprinklers work well when you use the restrictors on them to reduce the range. This breaks up the single stream coming out of the nozzle into smaller droplets.

2. Set the sprinkler in a central location in your garden. Use multiple sprinklers if necessary to cover the entire area you want to protect from frost.

3. Don't turn on the sprinkler until the evening or until you think the temperature is going to start dropping.

4. Place a bucket or pan in the garden near the irrigation to gauge how much water was applied to the garden. After you have put down 2 to 3 inches of water, you will risk damage from too much water, so don't use this system for more than a few nights.

5. Turn the water off as soon as the threat of freezing has passed.

OCTOBER
The Fruits of Our Labor

October is a transitional month filled with mixed emotions: a month of rest and reflection, celebration, and a time to imagine the next chapter. For me, a type of grieving accompanies this month, a recognition that another year has passed and that summer is over. But in other ways the arrival of October is a long-anticipated relief. As the intensity of the season culminates, I let go of any regrets and anxiety and allow that energy to slowly shift into planning for the next year. Along with the fall festivals and canning parties, we also celebrate peak seed harvest season. As the abundance of the garden reaches its zenith, so too does the collection and processing of the seeds we'll need for next spring's planting. Connecting the abundant fall harvest with the promise of next year's garden has always been a joy.

◄ Learning to cure and store winter squash correctly will keep you in veggies all winter long.

TO DO THIS MONTH

PLAN

- Record details such as first frost and rain amounts in journal.
- Prepare for frost: listen to the forecast.
- Indoor gardening: continue with herbs and microgreens.

PREPARE AND MAINTAIN

- Check and maintain stored crops.
- Clean and store winter squash.
- Turn off water and drain hoses.

SOW AND PLANT

Everyone

- Plant under cover: beets, carrots, kale, salad greens, and Swiss chard.

Zones 5 and 6

- Finish planting garlic.

HARVESTING NOW

- arugula
- beets
- bok choy
- broccoli
- Brussels sprouts
- carrots
- frisée
- kale
- kohlrabi
- leeks
- lettuce
- parsley
- parsnips
- potatoes
- radicchio
- radishes
- salad greens
- scallions
- shallots
- Swiss chard
- turnips
- winter squash

Zone 4 Zone 5 Zone 6

their starches into sugars in order to survive longer in the harsh conditions. If you haven't noticed this, or you have not harvested after it starts frosting outside, I suggest paying close attention and trying those post-frost vegetables. I have experimented with growing in hoop houses for several years, and nothing is sweeter than the spinach we grow through the winter. It almost makes me not want to eat it any other time of year.

A light frost is considered to be in the range of 28 to 32°F, whereas a hard frost occurs when temperatures drop below 28°F. Both types of frost will affect the plants growing in your garden.

One change to consider, especially if you are pushing the season, is that as soon as the hard frosts come, the pollinators stop their work. They hibernate, die, or live off the larder they have created. I have been tempted in the past to do a late zucchini planting, or push other summer crops into fall, but in many cases, this can't be done without pollinators. In professional greenhouses, they often purchase mason bees and other pollinators in the off-season, but that probably isn't practical for the home gardener. So, plan to finish up with flowering crops that require pollination by the end of October, or maybe even a little sooner, because the bees that linger get lazy in the cold.

The First Frost

October means the end of the traditional growing season. If you still have crops in the ground or in hoop houses, growth is now really starting to slow down—but it is not over. Often my last patch of cauliflower or broccoli will slowly size up during the warmer fall days and I can keep harvesting into November or occasionally December. I am always grateful for slow, warm fall seasons, but more often than not we get a freeze and everything comes to a halt.

An upside to colder weather is that some plants react to and engage defenses at the first light frost. Brassicas like kale, broccoli, and Brussels sprouts become sweeter. Some savvy farmers' market customers know this and they won't start buying these items until after the first frost. It turns out that sugar is nature's anti-freeze. The plants turn

Frosty Harvests: Dos and Don'ts

Observation and patience come into play once again when harvesting in the fall. After a frost, it can be a little tricky to know what is damaged and what is still okay. The images and smells on the mornings of those first

TYPICAL FROST TOLERANCE OF VEGETABLES

DAMAGED BY LIGHT FROST	TOLERATES LIGHT FROST	TOLERATES HARD FROST
beans	arugula	broccoli
cucumbers	beets	Brussels sprouts
eggplants	cauliflower	cabbage
peppers	celery	carrots
pumpkins	kohlrabi	kale
summer squash	lettuce	leeks
tomatoes	peas	onions
winter squash	radicchio	parsnips
	radishes	spinach
	Swiss chard	turnips

frost days are powerful. It is clear that something has changed. The grass crunches, it is usually quieter than normal because insects are dormant or dead, and evidence is everywhere in the form of white ice crystals. On the farm, we take time to observe and decide how hard the frost was and whether we think everything will die or just some things. As the day goes on, the sun comes out, the temperature rises above freezing, and we find out. Usually the first frost means just the tops of plants get burned, and some areas of the farm are untouched by the protection being close to the woodlot provides. By the end of the day, wilting has begun and we can assess the damage. Leaves droop, turn dark green

or black, and a post-frost smell permeates the air. The smell is hard to describe, maybe like the smell of an old freezer; in my mind it is the smell of plant death.

Because it is so hard to know how pervasive the frost was, I always wait to harvest until later in the day when plants have thawed, even with hardy crops like spinach and kale. This is the opposite of harvesting early in the morning in August when the concern is getting plants out of the garden before it gets too hot. The heat from your hands quickly thawing the leaves will cause bruises and damage. If you let the leaves of hardy plants sort out the frost on their own, while connected to the plant, they will be okay.

THE LAST FEW BITES!

It can be hard to let go of summer's bounty, but luckily there are a few ways to extend the fruit season besides row covers and hoop houses. If you think that the first frost is coming, do a "frost pick" to salvage the last ripe and almost-ripe fruits. Then experiment with the following simple methods for stretching out the season.

Boxing. Choose tomatoes that are nearly full grown and have almost no blemishes. Rinse them off with water, peroxide, or a little bleach to kill the surface bacteria and lower the chances of disease. Thoroughly dry the tomatoes, wrap them individually in newspaper, and store them in a box one layer deep. Check periodically to make sure that the wrapped tomatoes are not rotting. Within 3 to 4 weeks they should be ready to eat.

Hanging. This drying technique works to ripen tomatoes as well as to ripen and dry peppers. Leaving peppers and tomatoes on the vine will let them mature and age more slowly, and they will be more flavorful than those removed from the plant. It is a little messy, and you will need some space in a garage or basement where it won't freeze. Select plants that still have a lot of fruit on them. Pull them out of the ground, roots and all, and shake off the soil. Next, hang the plant upside down from a ceiling hook with twine. For peppers, let them shrivel and dry before untying the plant and removing the fruit. For tomatoes, the fruit will slowly ripen, and you can use the fruit until it is gone. The smaller, more immature fruit may not fully ripen, but give them time and see what happens. You can always make fried green tomatoes!

When it comes to fruits that are still on plants, wait a day to see what they look like. Part of what happens when vegetables freeze is that the plant cells burst and release water. Usually you will notice a soft, watery spot on peppers and tomatoes, in addition to the skin becoming a little translucent. But fruits that are still well covered with leaves will often be fine. If you really want those last few fruits, it is worth spending the time to search and sort.

I hope that before the first hard frost you have harvested all the root crops you want to store. If not, beware as you harvest. Freezing can damage the tops of turnips and radishes, as well as potatoes that are near the surface. It is difficult to tell if potatoes have been damaged until they go soft and rot. (Rotten potatoes are nauseating, so avoid this if possible.) Turnips and radishes are easier. Slice one in half: if a portion of the root is translucent or discolored this is usually a sign that frost has hit. You can cut off the affected parts and eat the rest of the root, but they are not worth storing at this point.

NOVEMBER
Looking Back on the Season

When daylight saving time ends and the clock says the sun is setting an hour earlier, it reminds me that the days are in fact getting a lot shorter. It is time to pull back, stop rushing, and relax a little. At first, I wonder what to do with that extra time between sunset and bedtime, but eventually I figure it out, filling it with reading, writing, and more time with my kids.

Each season brings with it another layer of understanding. You will observe more details about how plants grow, what makes them thrive, and how the seasons alter them. This slow compilation of observed details is a rewarding aspect of being a gardener. You are building a database around a microcosm that no one else will ever completely understand, and that is difficult to communicate. It is something that can only be built by hours in your own garden. This is your own special knowledge to cherish.

◄ **Crops like cabbage happily survive a light frost, providing you with a late-season harvest.**

TO DO THIS MONTH

PLAN

- Document fall garden layout in your journal or with pictures.
- Continue indoor gardening with herbs and microgreens.

PREPARE AND MAINTAIN

- Check and maintain already stored crops.
- Clean tools and store.
- Put away trellising materials.

SOW AND PLANT

Zone 6 ▬▬

- Plant garlic (early in the month).

HARVESTING NOW

- bok choy
- broccoli
- Brussels sprouts
- cabbage
- carrots
- chives
- frisée
- kale
- kohlrabi
- lettuce
- parsley
- radicchio
- radishes
- salad greens
- scallions

▬▬ Zone 4   ▬▬ Zone 5   ▬▬ Zone 6

Remove any crops with continual pest problems from the garden instead of tilling them in. If your tomatoes had blight or anthracnose, for example, pull the entire plants and put them in their own pile in a corner of your yard, or better yet, send them out in a yard waste container to a municipal facility. We often dispose of our tomato plants in a spectacular end-of-season bonfire. One consolation of growing in a northern climate, specifically zones 6 and lower, is that freezing temperatures kill the spores that spread many diseases. The freeze also keeps insect populations in check. On those cold winter days, when a garden seems like an impossibility, be comforted by the cleansing effect of winter.

Cover the garden in one way or another before winter. We have talked about mulching bare ground, cover cropping open areas, and intercropping between fall crops so a cover is already in place. These are all great practices and important for protecting and building soil. Although it may seem heretical, I also like to leave a few areas open, tilled, and ready to plant. The idea is to turn over the soil and let the freezing and thawing prepare the ground for spring planting, while also incorporating necessary amendments.

It is somewhat controversial in the sustainable farming community as it exposes soil to erosion from wind and water, but I also understand what spring is like and how many activities need to be done all at once. It takes some time in the spring for cover crops and mulches to break down and make way for plantings, so having a "clean" area available right away in the spring always feels like a relief and a blessing. Of course, gardens are more manageable than farms, so if it is not an issue for you, cover everything.

Closing Down Chores

With Thanksgiving around the corner and snow in the near future, it is time to clean up in earnest. Soon the cold will make you more inclined to retreat inside and fill your calendar with non-gardening activities. Whatever I don't get cleaned up in November will probably have to wait until spring. Before I really clean up though, I like to draw a rough map of the garden for crop rotation. Usually, enough evidence remains in spring to know where many of the previous year's crops were planted, but it is easier to remember and see now. It is especially important for main-season crops like potatoes, squash, tomatoes, and peppers.

Tool Cleaning, Organization, and Storage

▲ By leaving a few garden areas open and tilled, you can turn over the soil and let the freezing and thawing prepare the ground for spring planting.

Fall is a great opportunity to catch up on cleaning and organizing your tools. If you are anything like me, some tools and supplies simply get left where they were last used until they are needed for the next task. Collect everything in your shed or garage so you can see what you have, what's missing, what's broken, and what needs attention. Create a space for your tools, such as hooks on the wall of your shed or garage. You will be more likely to return them to that spot, and more likely

to find them there the next day. Over time on the farm, we built a few racks with labels for tools. More importantly, we bought a coarse bristle brush and a wire brush and hung them near the tools. Our system was that a tool didn't go back onto the rack unless it had been cleaned, which mostly worked—aside from the days when we worked too hard too late, and cleaning was the last thing we wanted to do. November is the time to take care of those tools that never got cleaned.

SHARPENING TOOLS

In addition to cleaning and organizing, the off-season is a good time to take your tools to a hardware shop for sharpening, or you can do it yourself. I have found a few simple methods for sharpening that I really like.

Shovels. Shovels are not meant to be razor sharp, but when they lose their edge they require considerably more effort to cut through sod. The solution is to use a 1-inch-wide file with a decently long handle. Find which edge of the shovel has a bevel, and follow that bevel with a long stroke, pulling the file toward you. If the shovel has completely lost any sign of a bevel, create one that is around a ¼ inch long. Your goal is a sharp point rather than a thin razor edge.

Hoes and harvesting knives. I use collinear hoes with replaceable blades and a simple 8-inch stainless steel knife with a plastic handle for harvesting. Because the knives tend to get lost over time, and the hoes have replaceable blades, and both of them get used for things they are not meant for on occasion, I don't sweat the sharpening process that much, and I don't want it to take a lot of time. My solution has been an AccuSharp tool that has a plastic handle and two small carbide tungsten bits in a "V" shape. This inexpensive sharpener works well, but it does take a lot of steel off as it sharpens. So don't use this sharpener on a good knife that you plan to have for a lifetime.

Other specialty tools. I recommend bringing specialty tools and mower blades to someone who has a lot of experience, unless it is a skill you want to master. Professionals use stones and steel to get the job done.

Metal tools with soil melded to them will slowly rust and disintegrate. A coarse brush works well to clean shovels, forks, and hoes, but for the chunks of soil, sand, and clay that end up like cement, you will need a wire brush. If you happen to have a particularly rusty spot on a tool, or a completely rusty tool, reach for a little WD-40. Use 100-grit sandpaper to smooth out the rough spots on tool handles. You can also oil the wood after sanding to keep it from drying out and warping or cracking. I have never had to this with the constantly used hoes on the farm: the sweat and oil from our hands is enough to preserve the wood. Once tools are scraped clean and ready for a few months of rest, put them on their racks or stack them in the corner—just keep your snow shovel handy.

DECEMBER
Rest and Recuperation

The short days of winter and cold temperatures naturally lend themselves to slowing down. I truly love the seasonality of being a farmer and gardener in the Midwest. Once December arrives, my thoughts become focused on the holidays and time with family. This space between the past season and planning for the next is a rare period of time best used for rest, reflection, and recuperation. Some gardeners in the southernmost parts of Michigan may still be harvesting a little, and others may be extending the season with row covers and hoop houses, but everyone has slowed down. As you consider this past season and start to look forward, imagine how you want to change your garden in the future and how much time you want to set aside for it. Gardening is hard work, but it is also joyful work; create a calendar for yourself that leaves room for joy.

◀ While your garden is resting, take some time to do the same. Reflect on your successes, and plan for next year.

TO DO THIS MONTH

PLAN

- Take a break and give yourself some time to recuperate!

PREPARE AND MAINTAIN

- Keep your eye on stored crops.
- Keep up with microgreens and herbs if you wish.

HARVESTING NOW

- Brussels sprouts
- cabbage
- kale
- leeks

From hoop house

- baby turnips
- beets
- carrots
- frisée
- kale
- kohlrabi
- lettuce
- radicchio
- radishes
- salad greens
- Swiss chard

Zone 4   Zone 5   Zone 6

▲ Pea seeds are easy to save for next year. Let the pods dry on the vines before removing the seeds.

Reflect and Think Holistically

December is a good time to reflect on the season and think about what you loved about your garden and what you want to do differently next year because it was frustrating or didn't work the way you wanted it to. Maybe rabbits got under the fence you worked hard to build, or the tomato trellis didn't hold up the tomato plants the way you thought it would. Instead of looking at these problems as failures, see them as learning experiences and opportunities to try something new. I think of December as a time to reflect rather than come up with concrete solutions. You can work on that when the new catalogs arrive and you begin to lay out next year's garden in January and February.

When you think about problems you experienced, think holistically. Was it that you didn't have enough time, or the soil needed more amending, or the seeds you used were old or from a questionable source? Usually the problems are more systemic. As with our own health, a lifestyle change often has the biggest impact—if you have indigestion, for instance, you can take antacids or you can change your diet. The same is true with the garden. If a plant is plagued with many pest problems, you can spray it with an insecticide, or you can adjust how the plants are spaced, or experiment with amending the soil differently to promote health. Without feeling guilty or like you did something wrong, just meditate on the garden, knowing you did the best you could. Solutions will come to you if you give them the opportunity to show themselves.

At the same time, think about all the successes: how you kept the weeds in check, why your cucumbers tasted so good, and how prolific the peppers were. Sometimes it can be just as difficult to remember how you did something right, as it is to fix something that went wrong. Make notes in your gardening journal while you still remember the details of the season and revisit that information when you are ready to plan for next year.

Organizing Seeds

One small way to prepare for next season is to get your seeds organized. By the end of the season my boxes of seeds tend to be a disorganized mess. Now that the focus is indoors, it's a good time to sort through them. Spread them out on a table and see what you have. As you go through the seed packets, make notes in your garden journal about how certain varieties performed, how productive or disease susceptible they were, and how they tasted. If you really didn't like a particular variety for any reason, get rid of the seeds. Pass them along to a fellow gardener or consider attending a seed swap. Toss packets that contain just a few seeds or none. Separate and discard seeds that you know won't be viable next year, such as crops like onions that don't last more than a year or those that are already several years old.

When you've narrowed down your pile, make note of how many seeds of each variety you have. This will be incredibly helpful when you start ordering seed in January and February. Once you have taken all your notes and counted your seeds, put your seed packets in resealable plastic bags or repurposed canning jars. This will help your seeds remain viable by keeping them from drying out or taking on moisture. You can further organize your seeds by grouping families together. With certain crops such as tomatoes, I grow a lot of varieties, so I like to organize the seed packets (alphabetically if I'm feeling ambitious) in their own containers. I use storage containers with tight-fitting lids that are shallow and long, almost exactly the size of the average packet standing on its side. Place the bags or containers back in the box and store it in a cool, dark place with low humidity such as a cabinet, pantry, or your basement if it is dry.

Squash Seed Saving

You might think it's too late to save seeds, but if you have squash stored for the winter, you still have a chance. For centuries, we have been breeding and selecting vegetables for size, shape, color, flavor, and more recently for shelf life and shipping durability. Saving your own seed is your participation in that history.

I grew winter squash for the first time soon after moving onto our homestead. Space was limited, but I couldn't resist growing a few hills of my favorite variety. We always liked to bake a squash around the holidays to enjoy with family and friends. Eventually, we tried our hand at storing squash for use throughout the winter. Some varieties certainly kept better than others, but one year I had a squash that held up the entire winter and into the next year. I knew I had found something special! I decided to harvest the seeds from this long-keeping squash to grow again the following season. It is gratifying to save your own seed and squash is a great place to start learning the process!

STEPS:

1. Choose your favorite squash variety and select the biggest and most mature fruit that you have. If you have one that is molding or starting to rot you can use it, or just make dinner with the squash you choose.

2. To avoid cutting any seeds in half, crack open the squash instead of cutting it open, if possible. A gentle smash on the garage floor should do.

3. Scoop out all the seeds into a strainer. Rinse them under cool water and separate the seeds from the clumps of the stringy flesh until the seeds are clean.

4. Lay out the seeds on newspaper or paper towels until they are dry, which usually takes 24 to 48 hours. Using your kitchen counter will allow you to keep an eye on them.

5. Put the dried seeds in a resealable bag or glass jar with a tight-fitting lid. Label with the squash species, variety, and date. Store it along with the rest of your seeds and test the germination rate before planting.

Edibles
A to Z

Apples, squash, beets, carrots—nothing compares to the ABCs of your own vegetable garden.

PLANTING AND HARVESTING CHARTS

These charts provide *approximate* planting and harvesting dates for annual plants cultivated outdoors in the garden without protective devices. See the profiles of specific vegetables for more information about starting seeds indoors, and which vegetables to direct sow or transplant.

ZONE 4

CROPS	JAN	FEB	MAR	APR	MAY	JUN	JUL	AUG	SEPT	OCT	NOV	DEC
ARUGULA												
BEANS												
BEETS												
BOK CHOY												
BROCCOLI												
BRUSSELS SPROUTS												
CABBAGE												
CARROTS												
CAULIFLOWER												
CELERY AND CELERIAC												
CORN												
CUCUMBERS												

Planting
Harvesting

CROPS	JAN	FEB	MAR	APR	MAY	JUN	JUL	AUG	SEPT	OCT	NOV	DEC
EGGPLANT						Planting		Harvesting				
FENNEL							Planting	Harvesting				
GARLIC							Harvesting	Planting				
KALE					Planting		Harvesting					
KOHLRABI					Planting		Harvesting					
LEEKS					Planting				Harvesting			
LETTUCE				Harvesting	Planting							
MELONS					Planting			Harvesting				
ONIONS					Planting		Harvesting					
PARSNIPS					Planting			Harvesting				
PEAS, GARDEN AND SNAP					Planting	Harvesting						
PEPPERS						Planting		Harvesting				
POTATOES				Planting			Harvesting					
RADISHES				Planting		Harvesting						
SALAD GREENS					Planting	Harvesting						
SCALLIONS					Planting		Harvesting					

CONTINUED ▶

ZONE 4, CONTINUED

CROPS	JAN	FEB	MAR	APR	MAY	JUN	JUL	AUG	SEPT	OCT	NOV	DEC
SHALLOTS				�			■	■	■			
SPINACH				▪	■	■		■	■			
SWISS CHARD						▪	■	■				
TOMATOES						▪		■				
TURNIPS				▪	▪	■	■			■		
WINTER SQUASH						▪			■			
ZUCCHINI & SUMMER SQUASH						▪		■	■			

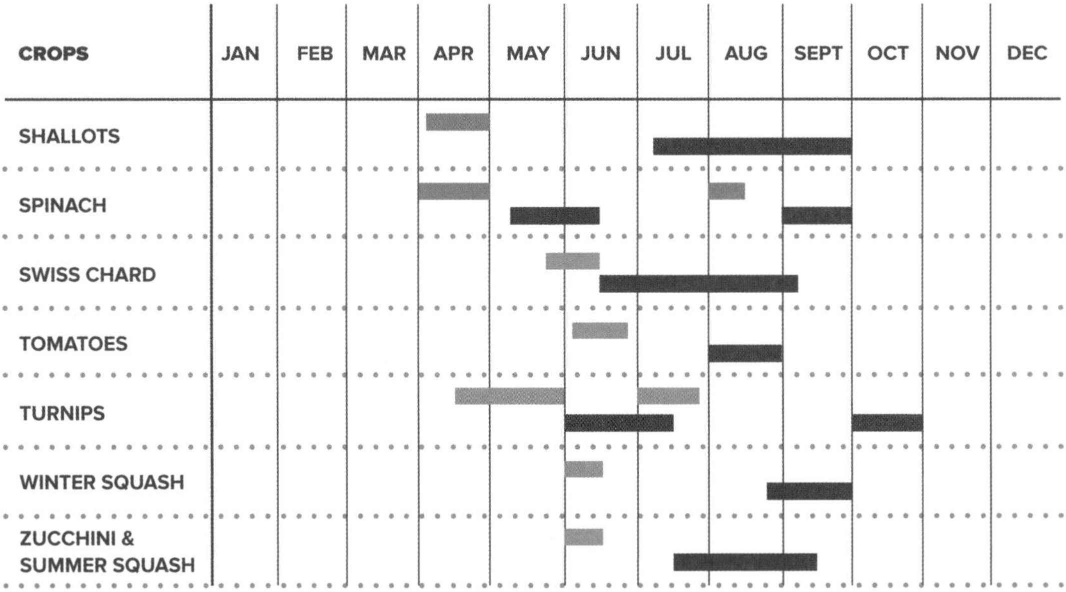

PLANTING AND HARVESTING CHART

Planting
Harvesting

ZONES 5 & 6

CROPS	JAN	FEB	MAR	APR	MAY	JUN	JUL	AUG	SEPT	OCT	NOV	DEC

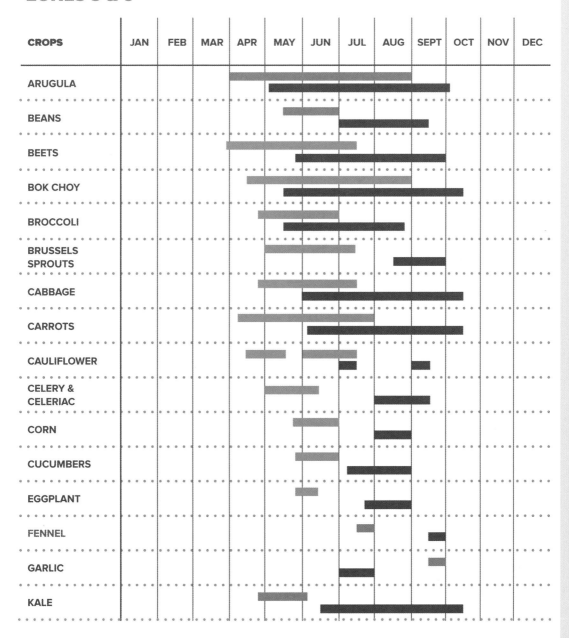

ARUGULA

BEANS

BEETS

BOK CHOY

BROCCOLI

BRUSSELS SPROUTS

CABBAGE

CARROTS

CAULIFLOWER

CELERY & CELERIAC

CORN

CUCUMBERS

EGGPLANT

FENNEL

GARLIC

KALE

CONTINUED ▶

PLANTING AND HARVESTING CHART

ZONES 5 & 6, CONTINUED

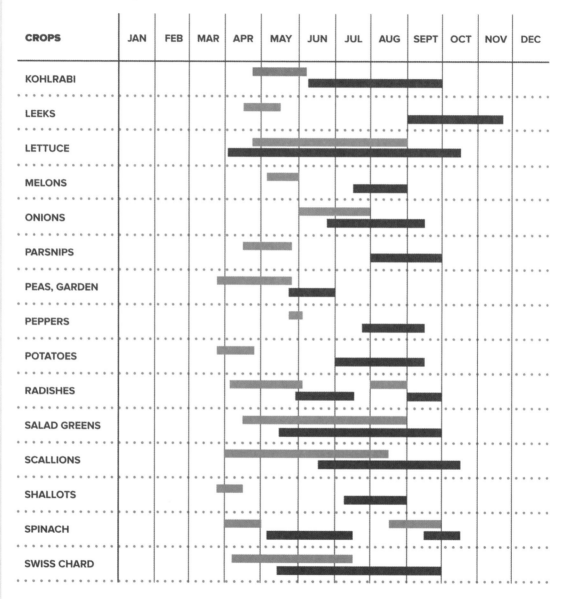

CROPS	JAN	FEB	MAR	APR	MAY	JUN	JUL	AUG	SEPT	OCT	NOV	DEC
KOHLRABI												
LEEKS												
LETTUCE												
MELONS												
ONIONS												
PARSNIPS												
PEAS, GARDEN												
PEPPERS												
POTATOES												
RADISHES												
SALAD GREENS												
SCALLIONS												
SHALLOTS												
SPINACH												
SWISS CHARD												

Planting
Harvesting

CROPS	JAN	FEB	MAR	APR	MAY	JUN	JUL	AUG	SEPT	OCT	NOV	DEC
TOMATOES					Planting		Harvesting					
TURNIPS				Planting		Harvesting		Planting	Harvesting			
WINTER SQUASH						Planting			Harvesting			
ZUCCHINI & SUMMER SQUASH						Planting		Harvesting				

Arugula

This peppery, leafy green has become a kitchen staple and an expected menu item at any self-respecting restaurant. The combination of meaty texture, heat, and spiciness means it can stand up to funky cheeses and balsamic vinegar without hesitation. This description applies to arugula grown in rich soil and not cut before attaining its full complexity of flavors. Mass-produced arugula that is smaller than your pinky and sold in plastic tubs is another thing entirely. Don't be deterred. You can grow great arugula.

GROWING A member of the brassica family, arugula is relatively easy to grow. Direct sow as soon as the soil is workable. Plant 4 to 6 seeds per inch into furrows spaced 8 inches apart and cover lightly with soil. Or broadcast seeds over the planting area; the thicker it is sown, the smaller the plants will be, so decide what size leaf you are hoping to achieve and experiment. Thin if needed and eat the thinnings. Sow every 2 to 4 weeks to have a crop all season long. Arugula is a heavy feeder and prefers rich soil; yellow leaves indicate that your garden soil needs nitrogen. All brassica salad greens are susceptible to flea beetles, which devastate the leaves with hundreds of tiny holes. The best defense is to place a row cover over the furrow before germination and pull it tightly along the edges.

HARVESTING The old way to harvest arugula is to let it get quite large, 5 to 7 inches tall, and make bunches with it. It is still occasionally sold this way and arugula that size is great for cooking. The new way is to grow it baby sized, 2 to 3 inches tall, at which point it tends to be milder. I prefer to split the difference and let it grow to about 4 inches. This size will give you the meaty texture and full flavor and will be great for both cooking and salads. To harvest, I cut around 1 or 2 inches above the soil, being careful not to cut below the part of the plant from which arugula will regrow. You can generally cut a patch of arugula once a week for 3 to 4 weeks in the summer, but in the spring and fall it will take longer to regrow. When after a few weeks a patch of arugula becomes a little ratty and the leaves gets tougher, start harvesting from a new patch.

VARIETIES The wild (perennial) arugula 'Sylvetta' has a strong flavor and uniquely serrated leaves. I recommend growing it only in the spring and summer. A wonderful cultivated variety, 'Astro', has been bred with a reduced desire to flower.

Asparagus

It requires space and patience, but once established, asparagus will provide you with years of spring pleasure. Cutting those spring spears at the perfect size and immediately eating them makes asparagus well worth the trouble. Including a few perennials like asparagus in your garden will give it structure, and it's nice to have some vegetables that you don't need to plant every year.

GROWING Although it is possible to grow asparagus from seed, most people grow it by using 1-year-old bare-root crowns. Avoid 2- or 3-year-old crowns because the transplant shock is more significant. Take time to decide where you want to plant your asparagus, as it will occupy that area for 10 to 20 years. The ideal garden spot will warm quickly in the spring and will have well-draining soil with a neutral or slightly alkaline pH. Begin preparing the bed as soon as soil is workable in the spring. Loosen the soil and dig a 12-inch-wide trench around 6 to 8 inches deep. Before you plant, soak the crowns in water to moisten the bare roots; add a little fish and seaweed emulsion to begin colonizing the roots with beneficial bacteria. Plant the crowns at the bottom of the trench, 12 to 16 inches apart, and cover with 3 inches of soil. As the plants grow, continue to fill in the trench with soil.

For the first 2 years allow the plants to grow without harvesting. This helps the plants focus on establishing roots that will produce vigorous growth in years to come. In the fall or early spring before new growth appears, cut the plants down to the level of the soil, and mulch heavily. Watch out for pests eating the fronds and control for slugs as needed. Top-dress with an all-purpose fertilizer each spring.

HARVESTING In the third season, cut spears for about 4 weeks, then let the plants mature. In the fourth season, you can expand the harvesting window to around 8 weeks. Snap off or cut the spears at ground level when they are 5 to 10 inches tall, depending on your preference. Crowns will produce about 1 pound of spears over a 6- to 8-week period.

VARIETIES Asparagus plants are naturally either male or female. Male plants are more productive since they don't have to spend energy on producing seeds. For this reason, choose varieties that offer mostly male plants such as **'Jersey Night'** and **'Jersey Supreme'**. If you want to have a little fun grow **'Purple Passion'**, just know that the purple color disappears when cooked.

Beans

Beans, which fall in the category of "most people like them," are an expected part of our Midwestern diet, especially combined with slivered almonds and situated on a plate next to mashed potatoes. Something about that "beany" flavor in fresh green beans is inimitable; when cooked well, I can never pass them up.

You can grow beans for their edible pods (green beans) or as dry beans and harvest them when seeds are mature. Beans are classified as either bush beans or pole beans. The main difference is that bush varieties produce shorter plants and begin producing earlier than pole varieties. The scope of the varieties I've grown over the years has expanded based on requests and catalog temptation. I suggest you branch out as well because growing beans really is a lot of fun.

GROWING I remember elementary school physical science lessons that involved growing a bean in a Styrofoam cup. This is not to say growing beans is all child's play, but with their big seeds and fast growth they are pretty easy and gratifying.

Directly sow bean seeds after danger of frost has passed. Plant bush beans in a sunny spot, 1 to 2 inches apart (about 1 inch deep) or broadcast seeds for a densely planted patch. They will bush out quite a bit, so I like to plant them in a 3-foot-wide bed to ease harvesting and reduce the risk of mildew and fungus by giving them a little room to breathe. Pole beans need something to grow on, such as a trellis or a teepee. Space seeds about 3 inches apart on the trellis or plant four to six seeds at the base of each teepee pole. Thin seedlings as plants show their true leaves; plant once a month for a continuous harvest. Be sure to plant dry beans on time in the spring, and patiently wait until the fall, as they take a lot longer to mature than fresh beans.

Beans need fertile soil and plenty of water or they will complain with yellow leaves and stunted growth. The biggest bean-growing challenge is the Mexican bean beetle, which appears first as a small yellow almost fuzzy maggot, and matures into a ladybug lookalike. You will likely notice irregular holes in the leaves. The best defense is to rotate the planting location of beans every year. Because beans are nitrogen-fixing legumes, rotating them will also improve the soil.

HARVESTING Beans mature quickly and when they start producing fruit they really crank them out. For green beans, harvest when the seeds are mature but not bulging out of the pod about three times a week. When harvesting, hold onto the plant while you pull the bean away (plants tend to have fragile roots so it is easy to accidentally pull the whole plant out of the ground). Beans picked when wet and stored will quickly mold. Avoid by harvesting when they are dry or use them right away. To harvest dry beans, let the pods dry out on the vine before picking and shelling. If they have not matured, they won't store properly or display their brilliant colors and patterns.

VARIETIES For bush beans, many people enjoy **'Provider'** or **'Dragon's Tongue'** The wide pods of Dragon's Tongue grow up to 9 inches long and are juicy and sweet with a refreshing flavor. They are cream colored with unique purple streaks that disappear when cooked. **'Romano'** is a green Italian bush bean that is substantially meaty with a strong bean flavor. **'Rattlesnake'**, a standout among the pole beans, is a productive climber with a unique flavor. The green color is streaked with some purple, which helps you spot them among their dense foliage when harvesting. The list of dry beans to try is endless; the more varieties you grow, the better! A good place to start is the beautiful **'Cranberry Bean'**. It is a common variety, so the seed is easy to find. One thing you will notice right away with growing your own dry beans is that they cook fast, and they are tender. You do not need to soak them for hours before using them.

Beets

Beets have undergone a renaissance in recent years, transitioning from much-maligned vegetables into sexy and desirable items at the farmers' market. Three things have changed the way we think about beets: how we cook them, the rainbow of available varieties, and the smaller size at which we harvest them. Instead of boiling beets to death, roast them. They'll retain their color and flavor, and with color and flavor come nutrients. A win-win. Sauté freshly harvested beet greens for a simple side dish or add the raw greens to soups.

GROWING Direct sow beet seeds in early spring, as soon as soil is workable. I tend to plant beets pretty close together, 1 or 2 seeds per inch. Plant about a ½ inch deep and cover with soil. When seedlings are about 4 to 5 inches tall, begin thinning (eat the thinnings!), eventually spacing plants 3 to 4 inches apart. Cut plants when thinning rather than pulling them to avoid disturbing the roots of other plants. For a continuous harvest, sow seeds every 3 weeks until midsummer. Take a break from planting during the hottest part of the summer and resume after temperatures drop for a late fall harvest. Provide beets consistent water and loose friable soil for their deep taproot. Overall beets have few pests and diseases. Fungal

issues with leaves can occur and nematodes sometimes affect the shape of the root, but neither really interferes with the end product. Keep the garden clean and weeded so mice don't take an interest in nibbling on the sweet bulbs.

HARVESTING Gently push the greens to the side so you can see the size of the roots. I generally wait for larger beets, but you can harvest baby beets as desired when they reach 1 inch in diameter. Hold the plant near the bulb and pull up, shaking off the soil. Rinse the beets off (outside if possible) to remove most of the dirt, then cut the greens off and use them as soon as possible. The bulbs will store well for a long time.

VARIETIES 'Yellow Cylindrical' has a nice yellow skin and nearly white flesh. Hard-working 'Detroit Dark Red' grows fast, develops a uniform shape, and has that classic beet flavor with just enough sweetness. Best harvested when around 3 inches in size, 'Golden' is a classic heirloom beet with a sweet and earthy flavor. 'Chioggia', an old Italian heirloom, has alternating rings of red and white (*chioggia* means striped in Italian). Chioggia is slightly less earthy and doesn't bleed much. Roasted, mixed together in a salad, and topped with a bit of goat cheese, these beets are unbeatable.

Bok Choy

Also known as pac choi, bok choy is similar to other Asian greens, but I think it stands out enough to get its own description. I love how it looks, how it grows, and the plant's texture in my hand as I harvest it. If you think you have never eaten bok choy, think again, as it is a Chinese food staple. The stalk is crunchy like celery, and the leafy parts wilt down like spinach. It is a versatile green that you can use in numerous recipes.

GROWING Start seeds indoors 4 weeks before last frost and wait until the danger of frost has passed before transplanting. Space seedlings about 8 inches apart with 12 inches between rows. You can also direct sow seeds about a ¼ inch deep and 1 inch apart. Cover with soil and thin to 6 to 12 inches apart when seedlings are 1 to 2 inches tall. Thinnings are delicious sautéed or fresh in salads. Sow every 3 to 4 weeks for continuous harvest. Bok choy is extremely susceptible to flea beetles; cover diligently with Reemay to avoid.

HARVESTING Harvest bok choy when plants are around 9 inches tall and when they seem to be filled out and have some substance; or harvest baby plants for aesthetics and tenderness. Bok choy is quite fragile and the outside leaves can easily crack. I position one hand gently underneath the plant and cut right above the surface of the soil. Then I turn the plant upside down and break off any torn or yellowing leaves (a natural occurrence on the bottom leaves of many plants) before trimming the stem back to the base of the plant.

VARIETIES 'Shanghai Green' is a beautiful compact plant that is reasonably bolt resistant, even in the summer. For some added color in the garden try **'Purple Lady'**, an incredible variety from China, which needs a little more room to grow but produces a taller and broader plant. Both are fast growers (45 to 50 days) and easy to manage.

Broccoli

Over the years I have attempted to get people to try unfamiliar vegetables with mixed success. It is a logical evolutionary defense mechanism that we don't want to risk our lives by eating something that might kill us or make us sick. But when I consider the plants that we humans have discovered are safe to eat, I wonder how we ever stumbled upon broccoli: a huge clump of flower buds. Whatever the reason, I'm glad we did, because it sure is a delicious edible flower.

GROWING Broccoli plants are fairly easy to grow, but getting a nice, tight, dark green head—like you typically see at the grocery store—can be challenging. This cool-season crop performs best in the spring and fall. In peak summer heat, broccoli grows quickly and wants to produce flowers, so the chances that your heads will be looser and generally misshapen are much higher. Slower growth in cooler temperatures will lead to tighter and more uniform heads.

In spring, about 6 to 8 weeks before your last frost date, start broccoli seeds indoors. Plant seedlings 12 to 18 inches apart; allow 3 to 4 feet between rows. This spacing gives them enough room to spread out and produce bigger heads (the heads will be slightly smaller if you plant them closer together). For a fall harvest, direct seed or transplant seedlings in midsummer. Broccoli is a heavy feeder and needs plenty of water. It also likes a decent amount of carbon in the soil so growing them in last year's mulch works well.

HARVESTING Timing is everything. Keep a close eye on your broccoli patch because it will go from ready to overgrown quickly. Heads usually start out a lighter green color and become darker green as they mature. The head is ready to harvest when it is full and firm (but the buds are still closed) and the florets have started to loosen or separate ever so slightly. Avoid waiting so long that the yellow flowers open because this will negatively affect the flavor. Most broccoli varieties produce side shoots after you harvest the main head. To encourage bigger side shoots, cut the main stalk down to four or five leaves.

VARIETIES In the spring I like to plant **'Calabrese'**. This is the classic Italian heirloom broccoli which matures quickly (60 days), produces nice side shoots, and performs reasonably well into the summer. For fall planting, **'Waltham 29'** (70 days) produces large heads and also produces lots of good side shoots. I have harvested this cold-resistant variety into December.

Brussels Sprouts

Like beets, Brussels sprouts have come back into fashion due to better growing culture and cooking methods. If you are not yet a fan, I recommend a slice of wood-fired pizza with Brussels and bacon to forever change how you feel.

GROWING Brussels are a long-season crop so it is best to transplant rather than sow directly. For an early fall harvest, start plants 4 months before first frost and transplant seedlings when they are about 3 inches tall. For late fall Thanksgiving harvest, transplant on the Fourth of July. Space plants around 16 to 24 inches apart with 4 feet between rows. Like most brassicas, the cabbage looper butterfly larvae plagues Brussels sprouts. If you have a lot of larvae, the sprouts can be easily ruined, causing several layers to turn brown. Bt is the best solution, sprayed weekly, until they are ready to harvest. Root maggots are best avoided through rotation.

HARVESTING Sprouts start maturing from the bottom of the stalk, so harvest the lower sprouts first waiting for the rest to fill in. Use a small paring knife to cut the sprouts from the stalk. If you want the sprouts to be ready at the same time so you can harvest the entire stalk at once, top the plants with loppers right above where the sprouts are forming. This tells the plant to focus on growing out instead of up. As with many greens and brassicas, the frost will sweeten them, so save some for a late fall treat.

VARIETIES Many commercial varieties of Brussels come treated with fungicide, many growers believe that untreated varieties simply won't produce good results in the north, but I disagree. I have had great results with **'Catskill'**, an older variety from the 1940s. (85–98 days). Another great variety is **'Long Island Improved'**, a semi-dwarf type that is perfect for the small garden. Red Brussels sprouts are pretty but challenging. Get them planted earlier as they need a good, long season to produce. Try the open-pollinated variety, **'Fallstaff'**, which is said to produce faster than any other red variety available at 102 days.

Cabbage

Cabbage is an iconic vegetable that speaks to the history of agriculture. It is a staple in many countries and the center of many ethnic cuisines. I can imagine cabbage growing alongside rutabaga in a peasant garden centuries ago; it is old, but it has never gone away. It grows fairly easily, produces a lot of bulk, and you can store it for long periods of time. The thicker and denser fall-storage cabbages are perfect for making sauerkraut.

GROWING In spring, start seeds indoors 6 to 8 weeks before your last frost date. Cabbage does well in chilly weather so you can transplant seedlings 2 or 3 weeks before last frost. I usually plant slightly smaller varieties in the spring, spacing seedlings 12 to 16 inches apart with 4 feet between rows. In summer, start seeds about 12 weeks before your first fall frost, and transplant the seedlings to the garden when they are 4 to 6 weeks old. I plant larger storage varieties in the fall; space plants 16 to 20 inches apart.

Cabbage needs the same things as other brassicas: lots of energy, carbon, and organic matter. Because cabbage produces such a big plant, it does a good job of shading out its own weeds (you'll still need to weed it once or twice, initially). Cabbage is susceptible to the larvae of the cabbage looper, but peeling back a few layers of leaves usually solves the problem. Weekly Bt applications are the best way to reduce the population if the infestation is serious.

HARVESTING To tell if a cabbage is ready, squeeze the head. If it is firm, the head is densely packed with leaves and ready to harvest. Push the head to the side and cut between the head and the rest of the plant; then peel back any damaged outer leaves. If a point starts to develop on the top of the head this means it is thinking about flowering so you better harvest promptly. The outer layers will often start to lighten in color to show it has matured too. You will know you are too late if the cabbage splits open. This can also happen to nearly mature cabbages if they get a large dose of water after a dry spell. You can still eat split cabbages, but do so promptly because they won't store well.

VARIETIES 'Red Express' is an excellent and reliable red cabbage. Savoy cabbages, such as 'Chieftain', take a little longer to mature but they are incredibly beautiful and make great summer salads. 'Early Dutch' is a fast-growing early spring cabbage that is excellent for summer slaws. The perfect cabbage for autumn planting, the cold-hardy 'Brunswick' is an incredible keeper and perfect for sauerkraut. 'Gonzales' and 'Super Red 80' are hybrid varieties that will produce mini-cabbages if you plant them around 8 inches apart. The firm, baseball-sized heads are really convenient because you can use the whole thing in one dinner and you don't have to worry about storing it.

Carrots

From Bugs Bunny to "stick used to shovel ranch dip into your mouth," carrots are culturally at the center of our diet. A carrot, fresh out of the ground (even with a little soil left on it), is also a perfectly convenient food. You don't have to cut, cook, or peel it before you can enjoy it. Carrots are a true garden treat.

GROWING Direct sow carrot seeds as soon as soil is workable. Plant about 30 seeds per foot, about ½ inch deep, with 12 inches between rows. Thin to 2 inches apart when seedlings are 1 to 2 inches tall. Plant every 3 to 4 weeks while the weather remains cool for continuous harvest. For a fall and winter harvest (carrots tend to have the best flavor in the fall after cooler temperatures), sow seeds about 10 to 12 weeks before the first fall frost. It can take 1 to 3 weeks for carrots to germinate; keep soil moist before germination and water plants well throughout growth.

Carrots need deep, loose, friable soil to produce nice long roots. Optimum pH is around 6.5. Although carrots will grow in a variety of conditions and types of soils, the more balanced and fertile your soil is, the sweeter the carrots will be. Prepare to weed (a lot) and thin plants. If you experience issues with nematodes—those microscopic pests that cause roots to become mis-shapen—rotation and fertility are the best cures. Rotating carrot plantings from year to year will also reduce incidence of carrot rust fly.

HARVESTING Keep track of which varieties you planted so you will know what size to look for when harvesting. To find out if they are ready, scratch the surface of the soil and check the diameter of the top of the root. If it is as thick as you are expecting, dig down a little further and pull the carrot up by the root. Don't pull the carrot up by the top because the tops can easily break off. If you garden in heavier soils, use a digging fork to loosen the soil. I like to push the fork into the soil several inches away from the carrots so I don't damage them. Remove the carrot tops right away; carrots will rather quickly become rubbery when tops are left on. Handle your harvest carefully as fresh carrots can be surprisingly fragile.

VARIETIES 'Rodelika' is an excellent variety, especially in the fall and winter, because of its nice size, quick growth, and robust flavor with a significant amount of sweetness. 'Mignon' and 'Caracas' are smaller and do well in heavier soils. Of the colorful carrot varieties, I have had success with 'Yellowstone' (best enjoyed cooked), as well as 'Kyoto Red' and 'Dragon' (delicious fresh or juiced).

Cauliflower

I have fond childhood memories of cauliflower—broccoli's slightly less popular sibling—slathered with cheese. The thought still makes me hungry. Homegrown cauliflower, crisp and fresh from the garden, doesn't disappoint either.

GROWING Start cauliflower seeds indoors, about 6 to 8 weeks before your last frost date. When air temperature reaches 60 to 70°F, plant seedlings 12 to 16 inches apart with 3 feet between rows. For long-season fall cauliflower, follow the planting information for Brussels sprouts. Cauliflower does not like the heat: it buttons, deforms, and turns funny colors as it switches from growing to producing seed. If you are having a hard time getting it to mature before it gets really hot out, you may want to focus your energy solely on a fall cauliflower crop.

Cauliflower has the same pests and needs the same care as broccoli, but here's the twist: in order to produce a stark white head of cauliflower, it can't be exposed to the sun. When the plants are large but before they've started forming heads, it is time to tie them up. Take the outermost three or four leaves and pull them up to the center of the plant. Using a piece of twine (rubber bands work too) tie the leaves in a way that will cover the center of the plant. Use just enough leaves to do the job, leaving the rest to work on producing the head. This makes it harder to know when the cauliflower is ready, but you can usually see what's going on by peaking in the side of the plant.

HARVESTING Cauliflower heads are ready after they have sized up and before they start to separate. They won't loosen in the same way broccoli does, but sections of the head will start to develop space between them when they are getting overgrown. To harvest, pull off the string you used to tie it, cut the head from the plant, and trim back the stem. Peel off any leaves that are connected to the head; leaves continue to respire and will eventually cause the head to become rubbery.

VARIETIES Two of the best open-pollinated, white varieties are **'Amazing'** and **'Goodman'**. Both of these varieties do well when planted in the spring or later in the season for a fall crop. A well-known, long-season variety is **'Olympic'**. **'Purple of Sicily'** and the yellow hybrid **'Cheddar'** don't need the same coddling as white cauliflower varieties, so they are worth trying. **'Romanesco'** is an old Italian beauty that looks nothing like traditional cauliflower. The mature head is a shocking chartreuse color, but the shape is the real showstopper. Its growth habit follows the mathematical rule of fractals, meaning it has infinite spirals within spirals. The flavor is bold and buttery; when blended it is silky smooth. To reach peak color, it needs sun, but it doesn't need to be tied up. Romanesco performs best if it can ripen in the cooler fall temperatures.

Celery and Celeriac

It isn't completely accurate to put celery and celeriac in the same category as their uses are completely different and they look nothing alike when mature. However, they do look similar as seedlings, they are closely related botanically, and they require similar care. Celeriac, also known as celery root, is a variety of celery cultivated for its edible root. Although the root is no replacement for celery's crunch, it is delicious roasted, pureed into a creamy soup, or mashed with potatoes. If you have to choose between the two, I recommend starting with celeriac because it is much easier to grow.

GROWING Start plants indoors 10 to 12 weeks before last frost. Keep seedlings above 70°F for the first few weeks and after that around 60°F. When nighttime temperatures average 55°F or above (planting when colder can cause bolting), transplant hardened-off seedlings into the garden. Space seedlings 6 to 8 inches apart, allowing 12 inches between rows for celeriac and 16 inches for celery. This will allow for sufficient air movement. Both plants are susceptible to many fungal and viral diseases as well as insect problems, but because you eat the root with celeriac, you have a better chance of success. The keys to beating celery diseases are weeding, keeping the plants dry, and growing in healthy soil. Plants need a lot of water to grow. Drip or soaker hoses are a better method than overhead watering, or water plants early in the day so they have enough time to dry out before night.

HARVESTING Celery is ready when the stalks fill out enough that you can imagine packing the ribs with peanut butter. Production of side shoots indicates that plants are getting past their prime. Get down on your knees so you can see the base of the celery plant and use a sharp knife to cut the thick stalk. Cut below where the ribs end so it doesn't come apart into individual ribs. Trim the bottom of the stalk as well as the top third of the plant. Save the flavorful tops for soup. Harvest plants before the first frost. I usually let celeriac grow until late fall. This gives the roots time to get as big as possible. They will tolerate some frost, but you should remove them from the garden before it freezes. Cut the plant right above the surface of the soil, or pull the whole plant and trim the roots when you have it in your hands. Trim the greens down (avoid cutting into the bulb) and use the backside of your knife to scrape the stubble until the bulb is smooth. Celeriac will keep in storage all winter.

VARIETIES 'Ventura' is a classic older variety of celery with grooved ribs and a darker green color. It is meaty, flavorful, and reliable. Lighter in color, the hybrid variety 'Tango' has smoother and slightly more tender ribs. A little flavor is lost for the tenderness, but not much. 'Brilliant' is the one variety of celeriac that I grow. When cared for well it will reliably produce softball-sized roots.

Corn

Nothing says "agriculture" like corn. It is the foundation of many civilizations, including our own, and in 2020 nearly 92 million acres of corn were planted in the United States. Most of that corn will be fed to farm animals, much will end up in soft drinks and candy bars, and some of it will end up in your gas tank. It is nearly impossible to avoid some sort of contact with corn in your daily life. But this corn is not the same corn you will want to grow in your garden and eat fresh off the grill. Sweet corn is bred from a spontaneous recessive gene and is harvested before maturity, as opposed to field corn, which is left to mature and dry out in the field. If you have the space, try growing it at least once, even if you end up with smaller ears or some earworm damage. The flavor of corn from rich soil is an enlightening experience.

GROWING Wait for the soil to warm before planting corn as the seed will rot and will not grow if soil temperature is below 60°F. A simple compost thermometer pushed a few inches into the soil will help you determine when to plant. Sow seeds 1 inch deep, 4 to 6 inches apart, and cover with soil. When plants are 2 to 3 inches tall, thin to one plant every 7 to 8 inches. Corn is pollinated by wind and pollination will be more successful if plants are closer together, so plant in blocks rather than rows. Instead of a single 30-foot row, for example, grow the plants in five rows that are 6 feet long.

Corn takes the phrase "heavy feeder" to a new level. It requires fertile soil, plus a significant amount of nitrogen. If you are gardening using organic methods, and feeding the soil instead of the plant, corn can be a challenge. I go beyond my usual application of fish emulsion and side-dress with composted chicken manure before it begins to produce ears (around the time the plants have six fully developed leaves). Once the ears are developing, and they start tasseling, the window for adding nitrogen is closed, and the plants will ride out their development with what they have available. Less nitrogen will mean smaller ears, but if your soil is well balanced and fertile, you can still have great-tasting corn. The corn earworm will leave the first few inches of an ear decimated. This is more of a problem in the marketplace as it is hard to sell corn like that. For home gardens, you can increase your chances of blemish-free corn without chemicals. Use an eyedropper or small spray bottle to treat the tips of each ear with a few drops of vegetable oil just as the tassels show signs of drying out. You can also peel the ear open slightly and physically remove any earworms you come across (close the ear back up with a clip or piece of twine). Earworms are most damaging to early and late corn because that's when their populations are highest; mid-season corn also tends to have husks that are tighter, providing better physical protection for the ear.

HARVESTING Judging when corn is ready to be harvested comes with experience. I usually feel the outside to determine if it is somewhat spongy, which indicates plump kernels. Tassels should be developed and drying out as well. If you think they are close, pull back the husk on a few ears and look at the kernels. When you find a perfectly ripe ear, make a note of what it looks like and seek out similar ears. Each variety and each year vary, so some sleuthing is usually required. To remove the ear from the stem, bend the ear down toward the stalk and snap it off. Eat as soon as possible as the sugar quickly turns to starch. Corn that is grown for popcorn, for grinding into cornmeal, or for seed should be left on the plant to completely mature and dry.

VARIETIES **'Golden Bantam'** (80 days) produces relatively tall 6-foot plants and has a pleasantly sweet flavor. It is reliable in the north and is usually ready in later mid-season, depending on how the spring goes and when it gets planted. **'Blue Jade'** (70–80 days) is a unique variety that only grows to height of around 3 feet and is an ideal choice for small spaces or even for growing in containers. **'Painted Mountain'** is the hardiest and most productive flour corn for northern climates and **'Dakota Black'** (85 days) is an excellent popcorn.

Cucumbers

When my cucumbers ripen in July, I eat my fill as I'm harvesting and add them to every salad and sandwich I can. Their juicy, crunchy sweetness is a great antidote to the heat. Fresh cucumbers from your fertile garden soil will change your perception from staple to something truly desirable. Cucumbers are also just a few simple steps away from becoming pickles or relish. In fact, many cucumbers are pickled and many older growers call raw cucumbers "pickles"!

GROWING Cucumbers have relatively short vines compared to squash and melons, so they can be planted closer together. My preference is to transplant the season's first crop of cucumbers so they can get a head start against weeds and cucumber beetles. If doing so, start seeds 2 weeks before last frost and set out seedlings 8 inches apart when they are 3 to 4 weeks old. You can also direct seed after the threat of frost has passed; sow in rows or plant three to five seeds on a small mound of soil. Allow 8 inches between the "hills" to give the vines room to spread out. Thin to 6 inches apart when plants show true leaves. Plan for two or three plantings per season. Keep plants well watered and plant these heavy feeders in rich soil. Cucumbers produce a strong vine, making them a good candidate for growing vertically in your garden. This saves space, provides the vines more air movement, and increases the likelihood of straight, blemish-free cucumbers. Harvesting is also easier because the fruit is more visible.

HARVESTING Cucumbers fatten quickly once they reach their full length. I like to harvest them when they still have slight ridges, just before their skin becomes smooth. They can be hard to see through all the foliage, so gently move the leaves around and look closely. When you find one ready to harvest, hold onto it, push the stem to the side, and snap it from the vine. Harvest pickling varieties when they attain the right size for your purposes, from tiny gherkins to bigger dill spears. Pickling varieties don't have to be used for pickling—they are also wonderful in salads. Cucumber vines will keep producing for several weeks, so harvest gently and keep them weeded. Harvesting when the vines are dry will reduce the spread of fungal or viral diseases.

VARIETIES The classic slicer **'Marketmore 76'** has a reasonable amount of disease resistance, nicely balanced flavors, and produces well in the north. The hybrid **'Olympian'** is a solid producer with a bit more disease resistance, but is slightly less flavorful. **'National Pickling'** was developed in Michigan around 1930 and it remains a top pickling variety. The plants hold up well through many weeks of harvesting and they have a nice, sweet flavor. Even though it is not actually a cucumber, I must mention **'Mexican Sour Gherkin'**, which is sometimes called a "cucamelon" (it tastes like a cucumber but looks like a tiny watermelon). It produces a vigorous vine with penny-sized fruits that you can enjoy raw, pickled, or in your favorite cocktail. The unique shape and flavor of the fruit makes up for the time it takes to harvest a quantity of them.

Eggplant

As varieties have become more available, attractive, and less bitter, eggplant has made a modest foray into American gardens and kitchens. Be liberal with oils when you cook to deepen the eggplant flavor and help it absorb other flavors. Seek out new recipes and cooking methods too, like roasting and grilling. Eggplant is in.

GROWING Eggplants need a long warm season, so if you are in zones 4 and 5, it may be helpful to transplant a little early under a hoop house or row cover. Start seeds indoors 6 to 8 weeks before first frost and wait to transplant until all danger of frost has passed and soil temperature reaches 60°F. Space these large plants 18 to 24 inches apart with 3 feet between rows so they have some room to spread out.

As a flowering and fruiting plant, eggplants will need nitrogen as well as phosphorous. A balanced garden fertilizer applied about once a month should suffice. However, if your soil tests show low levels of phosphorus, supplement by adding rock phosphates when you put the garden to bed in the fall or bone meal in the spring. The Colorado potato beetle and flea beetles are eggplant's main pests. Cover young eggplants with a row cover in spring, which is when flea beetles are generally the worst. The best protection from potato beetles is to plant them as far away as possible from where eggplants and potatoes were grown the previous year.

HARVESTING If eggplants are overgrown, they will become bitter, so watch for firm, glossy skin, a sign of ripeness. Size is also important. Make note of the mature size listed for each variety and harvest them when a little smaller than that or even at the baby stage. Sometimes I am able to snap eggplants from the vine, but I often need to snip them with pruners, especially to avoid damaging the plant. Beware prickly stems!

VARIETIES 'Black Beauty', the classic black Italian eggplant, produces glossy, blemish-free fruits reliably in the north. Harvest them around softball size to reduce the bitterness that comes with larger fruits. 'Listada de Gandia' is an old European variety from the mid-1800s with purple and white streaks on relatively thin skin. Asian 'Pingtung Long' is a beautiful, pink, elongated fruit, roughly shaped like a banana. I love slicing, grilling, and putting this variety on sandwiches. It is tender and doesn't usually become bitter. Harvest at around 9 to 10 inches long. 'Casper' is an all-white variety that is a reliable producer in northern climates.

Fava Beans

Fava or broad beans are an ancient species that has been cultivated for thousands of years. They have been used to improve soil by fixing nitrogen, to prevent erosion, for animal feed, and also for human consumption. These tough, hardy plants are easy to grow and are a welcome addition to spring harvests.

GROWING Plant fava beans in spring at the same time you plant peas. You can also plant them in fall, similar to garlic. They prefer cool weather and tolerate frost. Plant the large seeds 2 inches deep and cover with soil. Space them 4 to 6 inches apart, in rows 18 inches apart. I recommend planting 2 seeds per hole, and thinning to 1 plant. Low germination is common with fava bean seed. Aphids are the biggest pest concern for fava bean plants, as they can inhibit growth and spread diseases.

HARVESTING If planted early in the season, fava beans will mature sometime in June. If planted later they may struggle in the summer heat and yields will be reduced. Harvest when the seeds are plump within the shell. The first mature beans will be near the bottom of the plant. Cut beans from the plant so you don't damage the stem.

VARIETIES 'Windsor' is the classic reliable producer of large beans. **'Vroma'**, the improved version of Windsor, is more heat tolerant and could work as a second succession. The reliable heirloom **'Aquadulce'** is similar to Windsor, although with slightly smaller beans. **'Sweet Lorane'** is traditionally used as a cover crop for fixing nitrogen, but is also edible. The downside is that the beans are much smaller, meaning more work to create a meal from them. Nevertheless, it can be a fun experiment, and even if you don't eat many, you are still improving the soil. If planting this variety, find a supplier that specifically sells fava bean seed for cover crops, as the seed can be expensive in small quantities.

Fennel

I would grow bulbing or Florence fennel solely for its beauty—the firm, stark-white bulb, and the gorgeous, pale green, delicate, fernlike fronds stand out in any garden—but lucky for us it is also delicious. You can harvest fennel at the baby size, roast it whole, and set it alongside any number of dishes to beautify and enhance a meal. Every part of this plant, including the seeds, has found its way into a broad range of Mediterranean dishes. Fennel contains the same chemical compound as anise, giving it that familiar licorice flavor.

GROWING To get an early start in spring, sow seeds indoors 4 to 6 weeks before last frost and transplant fennel (or direct sow) after the threat of frost has passed. In sun and rich soil, space seedlings 6 to 8 inches apart with 12 inches between rows. Or direct sow 6 to 10 seeds per foot, cover lightly with soil, and later thin to appropriate spacing. Beware when timing your succession plantings—if fennel is caught in midsummer heat it will quickly flower; this may encourage you to harvest at the baby size. As a cooler-season crop, fennel often produces better large bulbs when planted in late summer for fall harvests. Providing sufficient water is the main concern and fall plantings will receive more natural moisture. Although it is a perennial in zones above 6, it is mostly grown as an annual for producing and harvesting the bulb. Fennel does well with monthly applications of basic gardening fertilizer.

HARVESTING I like to harvest baby fennel when the bulb is around 1 to 2 inches wide and 2 to 3 inches tall. A full-grown bulb is closer to 4 inches wide and 5 inches tall. I use my little serrated red knife to cut the plant just below the bulb. The fronds droop quickly, so refrigerate right away.

VARIETIES Forming a slightly flatter bulb, **'Zefa Fino'** is the most productive and forgiving variety. **'Orion'**, an F1 hybrid, is capable of larger yields than Zefa but is slightly less reliable and forgiving. Both varieties take about 80 days to mature.

Garlic

Garlic comes in two categories: softneck and hardneck. Only hardneck varieties regularly produce a stalk with bulblets, sort of the garlic flower, which you can harvest when immature as a "scape" and use for cooking. Softneck varieties tend to produce smaller and more numerous cloves than hardneck varieties and may have a larger overall bulb size. I am more compelled to grow hardneck varieties because I like using the scapes for early season garlic flavor, and I prefer fewer and larger cloves when cooking. Hardnecks also prefer a colder and longer vernalization, making them ideal for northern regions. If you are in zone 6, you will have equally good luck growing hardneck and softneck varieties.

GROWING In your first season, purchase healthy garlic from a trusted seed supplier. Prepare beds in the fall, at least a month before the first frost, to give bulbs a chance to produce some roots before winter. Choose an area with good drainage and high organic matter content. Loosen the soil at least 6 inches deep and amend well. Choosing which cloves to plant is important as it determines how your bulbs will grow; large cloves from bulbs that have six to eight cloves are ideal. Separate

the cloves from the bulb and plant cloves 2 to 3 inches deep, 6 to 8 inches apart, with around 12 inches between rows. Position the cloves with the pointed ends facing up. Cover the bed with 4 to 6 inches of straw mulch to protect them from harsh weather. This will give you good weed control in the spring (garlic plants have enough vigor to push through the mulch). In the spring, once the plants begin to grow, amend with liquid fish and seaweed emulsion.

HARVESTING If you are growing hardneck garlic, harvest the scapes in June. Both hardneck and softneck varieties will be ready in late July or early August, depending on where you live. A sign of maturation is yellowing of the garlic leaves. Once this begins, the plants will die back entirely and go into dormancy within a few weeks. Pull them out of the ground before this happens or the cloves will begin to separate from the main stem as the plant prepares to spread out for its next cycle. To harvest, pull the stem from near the surface of the soil (as opposed to the top of the plant). If you eat garlic before curing, it will have a sharper and greener flavor; once cured, the flavor is deeper and more robust. Dry and cure your garlic in a cool, dark place, such as your garage or basement, for around 2 weeks. I like to spread the garlic plants in a single layer on a mesh surface, so air can move all around the plant. Leave the tops on during the drying process. When the tops have completely dried, trim them down to about an inch above the bulb. Place cured garlic in a paper or mesh bag and store in a cool, dry place (the less light and humidity, the better) with your other roots. With the right conditions and some luck, your garlic should store until spring.

VARIETIES Great garlic varieties abound. A few hardneck varieties I enjoy are **'Purple Italian'**, **'Red Russian'**, and **'Music'**. An easy softneck to try is **'California Late White'**, a widely grown variety that you have probably seen in grocery stores.

Kale

This darling of farmers' markets, smoothie shops, and health magazines has gone from obscurity to mainstream practically overnight. The brassica looks a lot like broccoli when young, but it is grown for its leaves and does not produce any sort of head. Kale is easy to grow, harvest, and eat (try it raw, sautéed, or baked). Also, once a patch is established, you can harvest from it for a few months, making it well worth its space in the garden.

GROWING Start seeds indoors 6 to 8 weeks before last frost. When transplanting, space lacinato and curly varieties about 14 inches apart and give Russian kale varieties around 21 inches. Once soil is workable you can also direct sow and cover with ¼ inch of soil. Because kale prefers cool weather, some growers find that they have more success by planting kale in summer for a fall crop. Kale needs an average amount of water and the same fertile soil as broccoli.

Kale's main pests are cabbage looper larvae and aphids. Bt will take care of a serious cabbage looper problem, but the aphids can be a challenge. Kale leaves have a lot of nooks and crannies and aphids prefer the underside. Although time consuming, spraying under the leaves with insecticidal soap, Pyrethrin, or horticultural oils will help keep aphids under control; alternate sprays so the aphids don't build up a tolerance. While Bt and Pyrethrin are both approved for organic gardening, releasing beneficial insects can be quite effective in closed systems like greenhouses—and they are worth a try outside, too.

HARVESTING Harvesting kale is a snap, literally. Hold onto the stem near the stalk and push down to snap off the leaves. I like to clean up the plant by snapping off any side shoots and yellowing and rough leaves that I know I won't eat. Those I leave on the ground for mulch.

VARIETIES Rustic, substantial lacinato varieties (also called dinosaur or black kale) such as **'Toscano'** hold up well when cooked, are essential for kale salads, and have an attractive dark green color that screams "health." These are most suitable for growing in spring and fall. **'Red Russian'** is the summer winner: it does not get bitter as quickly and tolerates heat more than any other variety. It is more tender, lighter green with a tinge of red, and it is a beautiful plant. I enjoy curly, crunchy **'Dwarf Green Curled'** and **'Scarlet'** in the fall and winter because they hold up extremely well in cold temperatures.

Kohlrabi

Kohlrabi, broccoli's strange cousin, doesn't fit into most people's ideas of what a vegetable should look like. It isn't a root, or a leaf, or a fruit: it is a bulbous formation at the bottom of a plant. But I love it and I think everyone should try it. Combining a radishlike spiciness with the flavor of broccoli and the crispness of jicama, kohlrabi is great shredded in salads or roasted with other vegetables. It is juicy and refreshing in the summer, and it can store for months in the fall and winter. And on top of all that, it is easy to grow.

GROWING Kohlrabi grows quickly and needs little maintenance. Start seeds indoors, 6 to 8 weeks before last frost, and transplant when frost danger has passed. Space plants 4 to 7 inches apart, depending on how large you want them to grow. Usually, one thorough weeding will do the trick with kohlrabi. For best growth and flavor, grow kohlrabi in the spring and fall. If you want to grow them in summer don't let plants get larger than 3 inches because they will begin to split and grow in funky shapes in response to the heat. Keep kohlrabi plants well watered. Although kohlrabi is

susceptible to cabbage loopers, flea beetles, and aphids, pest damage is usually limited to minimal discoloration or scabbing that does not usually affect the fleshy part we like to eat.

HARVESTING Harvest kohlrabi when it is around 3 inches in diameter: any smaller and it is hard to peel; any larger and you risk woodiness. A knife works, but pruners are better because the stem can be thick and tough. Tip the plant to the side so you can see the bottom and cut ½ inch below the bulb, then trim off the leaves. If you plan to store them, avoid cutting into the skin.

VARIETIES Two reliable hybrids are **'Kolibri'** (purple bulb, white flesh) and greenish-white **'Winner'**. Both varieties mature in about 45 days, are cold tolerant, and are resistant to splitting. Winner will hold up longer than Kolibri in the garden without losing flavor and tenderness, but ideally neither will be left for too long. For open-pollinated options try the cold-hardy **'Delicacy White'** or the sweet and tender, purple-bulbed **'Blaril'**.

Leeks

In the early spring when it is still cold out and we fire up the greenhouses, leeks are one of the first things we seed in flats. Most varieties require at least 100 days to mature, which means they aren't ready to harvest until the fall, effectively bookending the season. Leeks are like a more elegant and sophisticated onion with a beautifully mellow and fragrant flavor that I strongly associate with fall. Leek and potato soup with a rich broth is devastatingly good.

GROWING Because they take a long time to grow, between 90 and 120 days, an early start is essential. Generally, February to March (8 to 12 weeks before last frost) is a good time to start the seeds indoors. If you don't have a seed-starting station, or enough room, order bundled plants that have been field-grown in the south, harvested, and sent north. Transplant leeks when they are about 6 inches tall and space them 7 to 8 inches apart. Burying at least one third of the plant will help the white sections be as long as possible. Weeding is necessary because leeks grow slowly at first and won't be able to shade out their own weeds until they begin to mature. One solution to the weeds is mulching with straw, but only do this if you have enough fertility and nitrogen in your soil to handle the added carbon. Leeks need good fertile soil in addition to ample water.

HARVESTING Harvesting leeks in the fall is one of my favorite activities—until it gets really cold and I can't feel my hands! They will hold onto the ground with all their might so grab on tight near the soil and pull up the entire plant. If they don't budge poke a knife into the soil to cut some of the roots until they eventually give way. Then trim the roots down to stubble and peel away any damaged leaves around the stalk, leaving a bright white stem. My final step is purely aesthetic. Holding the leek upside down, I make a fast slice on an angle to trim the leaves. Keeping the leaves closest to the base a little longer, cut in toward the top of the plant leaving a triangle-shaped pattern in the leaves. When you are ready to eat them, the easiest way to get the soil out from the layers of leaves is to chop them up and rinse them in a colander.

VARIETIES Leek varieties fall within two basic categories: fall and winter. The fall leeks are greener in color and are not cold hardy enough to make it through a northern winter. My favorite fall leek, **'King Richard'**, is tough, reliable, pleasantly shaped, and early, which means that even if you have a particularly short season, it will still pull through. The hardier winter leeks usually have leaves with a blue tint and a good chance of still being alive in the spring. The gorgeous heirloom **'Blue Solaize'** produces a massive stalk if given enough time to mature.

Lettuce

If I could only grow one vegetable, it would have to be lettuce because of the (seemingly endless) variety of colors, shapes, flavor, and sizes. It is hard to believe that with all that is available, iceberg lettuce has long been the popular preference and only recently romaine has entered the fray. Yet another reason for and benefit to having your own garden!

GROWING To jump start your lettuce season, sow seeds indoors 6 to 8 weeks before your last frost date and transplant a few weeks before last frost. Or just direct sow at that time. Plant 10 to 12 seeds per foot and cover lightly with soil so seeds can get the light they need to germinate. When seedlings display two or three true leaves, thin to 4 to 6 inches apart. It is generally best to grow lettuce in the cooler weather of spring and fall, although some varieties have been bred to cope with the heat and not produce their flowers so quickly. If you have a slightly shady spot, or an area that seems to stay cooler and wetter, plant your summer lettuce there. If soil temperature hits 80°F or more, lettuce will not germinate; start seeds in flats in your house or garage instead. Rich soil is key for lettuce growth along with plenty of water, especially during the summer months.

Although stressed lettuce can succumb to several pests and diseases, great soil and a fast growing cycle mitigate most of these problems. Deer may be an issue, and they are particularly fond of the sweetest part: the center of the head. Physical barriers in the form of fences and row covers will be your most effective solution.

HARVESTING Harvest head lettuce when it feels solid and full (or if you are starting to have a problem with pests, disease, or bolting) by gently tipping the head to its side and cutting just above the soil. I like to trim the stalk and pull off any ratty outside leaves, which tend to be a little bitter, especially in the summer. To prevent wilting, harvest early in the morning or in the evening and get lettuce into cool water as soon as possible. You can harvest most loose-leaf varieties using the "cut-and-come-again" method. Simply pick the outer leaves (tear, use scissors, or slice with a sharp knife) while letting the center continue to grow.

VARIETIES **'Merlot'** is an heirloom leaf lettuce with a full flavor and a deep red color reminiscent of wine. Extremely cold tolerant, this is a great candidate for growing under cover in the spring and fall, but is not ideal for summer production. **'Pablo Batavian'** is a beautiful, crunchy, sweet bronze lettuce with a lot of resistance to the summer heat. **'Winter Density'** looks like a baby romaine lettuce head, but has denser Bibb-type leaves. It is easier to grow and matures faster than true romaine lettuce with lots of positive attributes including its flavor and crunchy texture. **'Forellenschluss'** (also known as **'Speckled Trout Back'**) is a beautiful heat-resistant heirloom romaine lettuce that forms a tall head, though less heavy than other romaine heads. The flavor is great and its speckles pop with a little balsamic dressing. Butterhead varieties are flat and sprawling, producing a tight tennis ball–sized head in the middle as they mature. You can (and should) use all the leaves, but the center is the sweetest. Butterhead **'Regina Di Maggio'** has a texture that melts in your mouth and leaves with the most pleasant lettuce flavor.

Melons

When my son was around seven, he insisted that if he were a farmer he would grow only melons. I find this completely understandable. When grown in balanced, healthy soil, melons are incredibly sweet and rich. This must be what the deer think, too, because they usually eat several, just as they begin to ripen. When melons are in season on the farm, the picnic tables during lunch break will be strewn with rinds and seeds. I can't think of anything more refreshing when it is hot out and you have been laboring for hours. It can be a little tricky to grow melons well in the shorter seasons and cooler temperatures of the North, but with the right varieties you can do it.

GROWING Just as with squash, I prefer to start melons 3 to 4 weeks before last frost in peat pots (to avoid disturbing roots when transplanting), so they can get a head start on weeds and pests. For best germination, do not plant until soil temperatures are around 70°F; to hasten soil warming, consider using black plastic. You can also direct seed once soil is warm enough. I plant three seeds, ¾ inch deep, at the base of small mounds or hills. Great soil that is high in organic matter is the trick to growing melons—and any crop that we grow for its sweetness. Cucumber beetles can be tough on melons as they emerge from the soil. Growing young melons under the protection of row covers can help protect them, while simultaneously warming the soil. If you use row covers, remove them when blooming begins so pollination can occur. Once started, melons are fairly trouble free beyond weeds and deer. Straw mulch or landscape fabric work well to suppress weeds.

HARVESTING Finding ripe melons is a little bit like dowsing, and I sometimes think I would have better luck using a stick to guide me! The first signs I use for watermelon are size, shape, and color. When I find a watermelon that looks like the catalog picture and fits the description, I move in for a closer look. Adjacent to where the watermelon attaches to the vine is a tendril, a curly growth on the vine, which will generally turn brown as the melon ripens. If you still aren't certain of its ripeness, tap on the melon gently. A thud usually means it isn't ripe, but if you hear a hollow sound, it is probably ripe. It is easier to determine if a cantaloupe is ripe. The first signs are if they look full-grown and are starting to take on a subtle orange hue. A ripe melon should slip easily from the vine when you lift it. Once off the vine I give it a good sniff and a little squeeze before adding it to the harvesting bin. If it's fragrant and slightly soft, I am pretty sure I have a winner.

VARIETIES As for watermelons, heirloom **'Cream of Saskatchewan'** has light green skin with dark stripes, white flesh, and big seeds. Harvest carefully because its thin skin easily cracks when fully ripe. **'Sunshine'** is a hybrid yellow-fleshed melon with skin that looks similar to Cream but does not split open as easily. It has smooth, but brittle flesh, and it ripens reliably. The classic heirloom red melon, **'Sugar Baby'**, has a strong, dark green rind that keeps it from splitting along with great texture and flavor. These three varieties are known as "icebox" melons because they can fit in your refrigerator without taking over; they weigh around 8 to 10 pounds. In the average (and even cooler-than-average) northern summer, they will all produce well. **'Charentais'** is a productive and sweet cantaloupe with a great floral smell. This classic French variety is considered a true cantaloupe, and it matures in northern gardens in anywhere from 75 to 90 days. **'Honeydew'** is a reliable, floral-flavored, green-fleshed melon type that is always a hit.

Onions

Onions are a worldwide commodity and have been incorporated into virtually every cuisine. They have a wide range of colors, flavors, and uses from raw to cooked to caramelized and fried. Although they can take some work to grow and maintain, it is rewarding to produce your own supply.

GROWING Onions take a long time to mature. If you are in zones 4 to 5, or want early onions, you have a few choices: start them indoors 8 weeks before planting them in the garden, purchase bare-root onion plants that have been started in fields in the south, or buy "onion sets" (immature onions that will continue to grow when planted). If you live in zones 5 to 6, you can direct seed onions. The biggest challenge with direct seeding is controlling the weeds because it takes a while before the plants are large enough to compete. They will also mature late in the season.

For transplants, sets, and bare-root plants, prepare the soil as soon as the ground is workable. Place individual plants around 4 to 6 inches apart; you can also group three or four plants every 8 to 12 inches (this can ease weeding). Rows should be 12 to 18 inches apart. If you are direct seeding, sow 10 to 12 seeds per foot, planting ½ inch deep and covering with soil. Thin to four or five plants per foot when they are 2 to 3 inches tall. Onions have few worrisome pests. Provide adequate moisture to ensure good bulb size.

HARVESTING Onions are ready to harvest when the tops begin to die back. Pull the entire plant from the ground and cure in a warm dry place out of the sun for a few weeks. Once they are dried, cut off the tops and remove any soil that is still on the bulbs. Keep the outer dry layer intact for storage.

VARIETIES My favorite storage varieties are yellow **'Clear Dawn'**, red **'Rossa Di Milano'**, and sweet white **'Candy',** although the latter is a hybrid variety. **'Walla Walla'** is a large, sweet, yellow onion not intended for storage.

Parsnips

For many people, the humble parsnip is considered a late season oddity that appears at their farmers market once the cool weather of fall arrives but in fact, this flavorful root vegetable has been enjoyed since antiquity. After trying it for the first time many years ago, I was quickly won over by the parsnip's smooth texture and rich flavor with just a touch of that earthy essence. Try it roasted or mashed for a simple hearty treat.

GROWING Parsnips have an incredibly deep taproot and enjoy a loose well-drained soil to spread down into; if blocked by hardpan soil they may grow short and stubby. Parsnips are not cold hardy as seedlings, so wait until after last frost to direct sow. Plant ½ inch deep, space ½ inch apart, and cover with soil lightly. They are slow growing and will need a few weeding sessions until they are established. Keep soil moist to speed germination and thin to 3 to 4 inches between seedlings. Once established, parsnips are quite hardy and they overwinter well; add them to the list of previous year's crops you can begin harvesting the next spring. Avoid carrot rust fly by changing the location of crops yearly or skipping years between plantings. This will also decrease the chance of canker (discoloration and eventually rot), which is caused by bacteria let in through damage from carrot root flies.

HARVESTING I like to wait until after the first frost to begin harvesting parsnips. The cold weather improves the flavor, adding sweetness and depth. Because of their long taproot, you'll want to get your shovel or digging fork ready. I dig next to the row to loosen the soil—far enough away to avoid damaging the roots, but close enough to effectively loosen the parsnips. You may still have to pull them out, but it will be easier. Once they are out of the ground, snap the tops off to keep them from getting rubbery, just like carrots. Parsnips will easily overwinter, so if you want a spring treat, leave them in the ground. In the spring, as soon as the ground thaws, start pulling them. If they begin to grow, the root will get soft as the plant puts all its energy into producing seed.

VARIETIES I have enjoyed growing the open-pollinated variety **'Andover'** as well as the hybrid **'Javelin'**. You can't go wrong with either variety, but Javelin is more resistant to canker and is considered by chefs a little more refined in flavor.

Peas

Peas mean spring. The large seeds push out of the ground like a figurative olive branch—a reminder that your garden will grow again. My childhood impression of peas was split pea soup, which I love, but I now know that this represents only a small fraction of how peas can be enjoyed. Snow peas in stir-fries, snap peas in salads, and freshly shucked English peas eaten like candy: their range is vast and unequivocally delicious.

GROWING Inoculating pea seeds before planting is inexpensive and worth the extra step. The bacteria help encourage pea plants to fix their own nitrogen, so they grow faster and sturdier. It also increases the amount of nitrogen left in the soil when the plants are tilled under in the fall. My inoculating process is to pour the seeds I am planning to use in a small bucket along with a dash of water and pinch of inoculant. Then I swirl the mixture until the seeds are thoroughly coated.

Direct sow peas as soon as ground can be worked. I plant thickly, around 1 seed per inch, and a little less than an inch deep. Keep soil moist until germination. Trellising taller varieties is essential for productivity and to ease harvesting. Place stakes around 6 feet apart and run twine horizontally between the stakes.

To reduce mildew, provide good air movement around the plants and avoid overhead watering. Straw mulch helps hold moisture in the soil (thus reducing the amount of watering needed) and suppresses weeds.

HARVESTING Each type of pea displays different signs of ripeness, and it is critical to harvest them at the right time so that the flavor and texture are correct. There usually isn't much of a window either, so visit the pea patch frequently and taste your way through the harvest. Harvest snow peas when they have immature seeds in the pod and are nearly flat but at their specified length. Snap or sugar peas should have larger seeds, almost a rounded pod, but not to the point where you can clearly see the individual seeds, which happens when the seeds are fully mature. English or shelling peas should have nearly mature seeds in the pod, but they need to be harvested before the sugars start turning into starches and the sweetness disappears.

VARIETIES Snow peas: **'Oregon Giant'** produces large plants and the peas are a little sweeter than the average snow pea. Sugar or snap peas: I have always relied on the classic **'Sugar Snap'**. Most snap pea varieties are very susceptible to mildew, and this variety is no exception. What I have found though is that when resistance to mildew is bred in, sweetness is bred out. My advice is to take care of the plants as best you can, and tolerate the mildew as you enjoy the sweetness. For English or shelling peas, I have settled on **'Lincoln'**: they produce big pods containing six to eight peas in each and the flavor is fantastic.

Peppers

Many people tend to think only of big green blocky bells when they hear the word "pepper," but after growing peppers in your own garden, your visual lexicon will change to include fruits of many varying shapes, sizes, and colors. Also, many people don't realize just how good peppers can be until they taste the nuanced fruity sweetness of a home-grown pepper, picked at its peak ripeness. Growing peppers is a compelling reason to have your own garden. You simply won't be able to find that kind of flavor anywhere else.

GROWING Sow seeds indoors 6 to 8 weeks before last frost. Don't let the temperature drop below 60°F when starting indoors or the plant will become dormant. Warm soil with black plastic before planting or use row covers. Transplant hardened-off seedlings 2 to 3 weeks after last frost, spacing plants 16 to 20 inches apart in rows 18 inches apart. Mulch peppers after they are established to keep them moist and weed-free. It is important to keep ripening peppers away from the soil. Taller varieties will benefit from staking.

To ease pepper growing, keep a few considerations in mind. First, soil should be amended with a nitrogen and phosphorous ratio that promotes flowering as much as it promotes growth. Second, thoroughly soak plants once a week so they develop a strong root system and the fruits can grow to their preferred sizes. Third, know that most pepper varieties need a good hot summer to really be productive. If you live further north, consider growing them in a hoop house or choose smaller varieties. The corn earworm and the fall armyworm can both cause some issues; Bt and garlic or hot pepper sprays (oddly enough) can help. Peppers are prone to the same viral and bacterial issues as other nightshades. Good air movement, no overhead watering, and healthy soil are the best preventatives; use hydrogen peroxide or copper sprays if the problems are widespread.

HARVESTING Patience is the key, especially with different colored peppers. Most peppers start out green and take on their mature colors as they ripen. Know which green peppers are supposed to turn colors and wait: it's worth it. Use pruners to snip peppers off the plant because branches can be surprisingly fragile.

VARIETIES There are so many amazing pepper varieties available to the grower that developing a short list of my favorites is a daunting task. **'King of the North'** is a great bell pepper for the northern Midwest. The fruit is medium sized and has nice thick walls, but it produces even in particularly cool summers. You can leave the peppers on the plant to turn red, but catch them before they are fully red, as they tend to overripen quickly. Long, slender **'Italia'** is meaty and has a deep, sweet flavor. Watch them closely because they start to get soft shortly after turning perfectly ripe. The plants can also be a little flimsy; mulch or stake them to keep fruit off the ground. **'Jimmy Nardello'** is smaller than Italia, but has an even more dynamic flavor. **'Spanish Spice'** is a nice frying pepper and is more spicy than hot. I am not a hot pepper fanatic, so I tend to stick with **'Early Jalapeno'** for jalapenos because they are big enough to stuff, along with highly productive **'Serrano'** and **'Joe's Long Cayenne'**. The hot pepper world is huge—if you are an adventurer, just play around. For the truly brave, I hear that **'Carolina Reaper'** peppers are where it's at these days.

Potatoes

Thinking of potatoes as a staple risks making them sound industrialized and boring, but they are rewarding and a lot of fun to grow. There are so many varieties to choose from and most are incredibly productive. It's a real thrill to plant half a potato and dig up ten at the end of the season!

GROWING Procure certified disease-free seed potatoes from a reliable source. I cut larger ones into quarters or thirds, making sure each piece has at least three eyes. Some people sprout them first or cut them a few days early to allow the cut flesh to dry. Allowing the freshly cut potato pieces to dry before planting helps to prevent diseases or rot. Plant potatoes 2 to 4 inches deep and around a foot apart in a 3-foot-wide bed. When they burst out of the ground after a couple of weeks, it is time to hoe. Hill potatoes when they are 8 to 12 inches tall by gathering extra soil around the base of the plants. This additional soil keeps potatoes, which tend to grow near the surface, from being exposed to the sun and turning green and bitter. (The green color indicates the production of solanine, a toxin that can make you sick.) If you have a small gardening space, you could try growing potatoes in pots or barrels with drainage holes drilled in the bottom and sides. Place some soil and seed potatoes at the bottom of the container and continue adding soil as the plants grow. You will end up with a container filled with potatoes. I have also seen people use tires: start by planting potatoes in the center of one and slowly add tires to the stack as plants grow. Potatoes have been grown for so long that they have attracted quite a host of hangers-on from potato beetles and wireworms to blight and scab. Potato beetles are wanderers: they do not have a good sense of where their host plant is and they fly off randomly when they mature. The size of most gardens makes it difficult to rotate crops far away from where they were planted last year, but the further away you can move them, the better. I also recommend buying new seed every year to reduce build-up of scab and other problems.

HARVESTING This is the fun part. Potatoes can be harvested once they flower; this is the best time to gather small, 'new' potatoes. small potatoes. You know when your potatoes have reached full size and are finished growing when the plants begin to die back. I am always curious about how they are doing so I will often dig around the edge of maturing plants to check their status. My harvesting method is to get on my knees, straddle the row, and gently pull up the plants; be aware that some potatoes may remain attached to the plant. I like to search about a 2-foot-square area, sifting the soil with my hands, and plunking the found potatoes into a bucket. If you have heavier clay soil, a digging fork may be required, just avoid spearing your tubers.

VARIETIES Medium-sized **'Yukon'** is great for baking and boiling because of its firm, drier texture. It is buttery and smooth when prepared. **'Cranberry Red'** is a larger potato with red skin and a pinkish tint inside. Its flesh is soft and moist when prepared well (try sautéing). **'Peruvian Purple'** potatoes are actually blue, inside and out, and similar to Cranberry Red potatoes in use and texture. Another must-grow potato is the long, slender **'Russian Banana'** fingerling with moderately dry, slightly waxy flesh and a rich flavor. Grow all four varieties and you will have a wide range of flavors, colors, textures, and uses.

Radicchio

I have been enamored with this beautiful, red-mottled, pleasingly bitter plant since I started gardening. Extremely hardy, radicchio is a great addition to any northern garden, and a gateway to other members of the chicory family such as frisée and endive.

GROWING Radicchio is slow to germinate, so I recommend starting the plants indoors. You can grow it throughout the season, although it performs best in the spring and fall. Start your first round 4 to 6 weeks before transplanting; plant seeds in pots or cells ¼-inch deep and cover with soil. Transplant in rich fertile soil as soon as the ground is workable. Space seedlings 8 inches apart with 12 inches between rows and water them in well. A lack of nutrients will show up as paler coloration and stunted growth. Radicchio is relatively pest-free, but in particularly wet areas you may experience some slug damage. Give the plants a chance to dry out between watering and keep the beds free of litter. If you struggle with deer munching on your radicchio, try covering with Reemay and hope that they won't tear through the row cover with their hooves.

HARVESTING Radicchio is mature when the heads become firm, typically between the size of a baseball and a softball. Squeeze a few to decide if they are ready. Some heirloom and less-refined varieties vary quite a bit in color and shape. Occasionally some plants never "head up" and will stay loose like lettuce.

VARIETIES Radicchio is either round (more common) or upright, like a small tight head of romaine. For the round type, try dark red, reliable **'Indigo'**. Upright **'Fiero'** has long deep red leaves that can be used individually to be filled with something savory. Both of these varieties are expensive hybrids. **'Palla di Fuoco Rossa'** is an older, Italian heirloom variety with all the radicchio flavor but more diversity of leaf color and shape.

Radishes

The red bunches amid a sea of green always add a lovely pop of bright color to the farmers' market display. When I was just a young boy, living with my grandmother in our third-floor apartment, radishes were the first crop that I ever grew. I planted them in a small window box on our balcony and I was thrilled at how quickly I was able to harvest and enjoy my little crop of spicy radishes.

GROWING Direct sow radishes as soon as soil is workable in spring as well as at the end of summer for a fall harvest. You can seed them thickly, but they will need to be thinned to around 6 inches apart to ensure that the radishes have enough space to properly develop. Since radishes are a quick crop, you don't need to fertilize them, but they do require plenty of water to grow nice-looking roots. I suggest succession planting them (every few weeks) in spring and fall when they will perform the best. Winter radishes should be planted toward the end of summer. In the heat some radish varieties try to flower right away, which pulls energy from the root and causes

deformed radishes. Most commercial radish seed is inoculated with insecticides and fungicides to deter pests and disease. Root maggots, which are spread by flies, are capable of destroying an entire patch of radishes post-haste. Another affliction it shares with fellow brassicas is the flea beetle. This will not affect the root, but it can slow their growth and make them less attractive. Cover radishes with a row cover before seedlings emerge to protect from both flea beetles and root maggots.

HARVESTING Standard radishes are only good when young—they get "pithy," fibrous, and hollow at the center, when overgrown. You will usually see the larger radishes crowning out of the soil; I take those first, but they will all be ready within a couple of weeks. Winter storage radishes take longer to mature and grow larger. They don't get pithy and fibrous, so you have more time. I have harvested winter radishes as large as softballs! All radishes get rubbery quickly so top them right after harvesting.

VARIETIES Of the standard red radishes, it seems that the most commonly grown variety is the uniform and reliable hybrid **'Cherriette'**. **'Pink Beauty'** is an heirloom with a soft pink color and is equally uniform and reliable. For a little excitement try the multicolored **'Easter Egg'** radish mix. This mix is quick to bolt so it can be difficult to grow in warmer temperatures. Also, the white radish in the mix is slower to mature, so near the end of the harvest most of your radishes will be white. Winter storage radishes include **'Black Spanish'** and **'Watermelon'** (originally from China, where they are also known as **'Shinrimei'**). Black Spanish can be piquant when eaten right out of the ground, but with time in storage they will mellow out. Watermelon radishes are less needy and incredibly beautiful when sliced.

Salad Greens

Many people are surprised the first time they experience the sweetness of fresh-picked greens. Of course, many people were surprised the first time their salad plate showed up with reds and ruffles mixed in with the greens. Most salad greens are quick growers that can be tucked in any available spot in the garden.

GROWING With some herbs and flowers, you can transplant seedlings, but most salad greens are best direct sown a few weeks before last frost. Plant seeds thickly and cover lightly with soil. Salad greens are fairly easy to grow and don't need much maintenance beyond weeding. Most weeds will not make you sick, but they can impart some awful flavors and textures into a salad.

HARVESTING The cut-and-come-again method works well for most salad greens. I let them grow to about 4 to 5 inches high and then cut the top 3 inches or so. This gives the leaves time to become sturdy and substantial and allows plants to develop a root structure that will help them regrow for another cutting. I try not to harvest more than three times from the same plant because after a while the leaves start to look a little rough and become tougher in texture and stronger in flavor.

VARIETIES Several catalogs offer premixed salad greens seeds. I have grown blends offered by a number of commercial seed companies but have also enjoyed mixing and creating custom mixes at home. Many of these salad blends are predominantly Asian greens, with kale and arugula added for texture and flavor. Other specialty salad greens include chervil, mâche, sorrel, cress, beet greens, kale, sea beans, and pea sprouts. The list goes on from there. Have fun, do some research, and experiment—you and your dinner party guests will never think of salad the same way again.

Scallions

Scallions are milder than bulb onions, but they are quick growers, easy to harvest, and tearless to prepare. Use in salads, stir-fries, and anywhere else you need that onion flavor.

GROWING Under Elliot Coleman's influence, I have started growing scallions in bunches rather than in a single row. It is easier to weed around them when they are planted this way. Scallions start off slowly and their seeds are tiny. Starting them indoors will give you more control and allow you to keep a better eye on them. I put 12 to 14 seeds in a 1- to 2-inch cell, 10 to 12 weeks before last frost. Transplant as soon as the ground is workable and bury about a third of the plant to get a longer white section. Onion root maggots are the most bothersome pests. Allowing scallions to overwinter can increase root maggot issues, so be sure to clean up your garden at the end of the season. Using a row cover at the time of planting or transplanting helps if you have a serious problem.

HARVESTING You can harvest scallions at any time. My preference is when they are around the width of a pencil, but some people like them thinner and others thicker. When you decide to harvest them, hold them close to the soil, and gently pull them out, avoiding any squeezing and subsequent bruising. I like to trim the roots right then and maybe peel back an outer leaf or two. Rinse them off and they are ready for the kitchen.

VARIETIES **'Evergreen Hardy White'** is an heirloom variety from Japan that is commonly grown all around the United States. **'Deep Purple'** scallions will provide a little color.

Shallots

After growing shallots one year I fell in love. Compared to the shallots commonly seen in grocery stores, I found their fresh greens and purplish skin stunning. And nothing can compare to that distinctive mild flavor.

GROWING Start shallot seeds indoors in early spring and transplant when seedlings are at least 3 inches tall. If you want to get a head start, you can use shallot sets instead of seeds. Sets, which look similar to garlic cloves, are immature bulbs that have been harvested and dried. Plant sets 4 weeks before last frost, spacing 8 inches apart. Alternately, you can grow shallots like garlic; plant in the fall for an early summer harvest. Shallots are relatively free of pests and disease. Mulch to help keep weeds down and moisture in the soil.

HARVESTING Shallots take around 100 days to mature; when started early in the spring they are usually ready for fresh harvesting in mid-August and fully mature by September. You know they are finished growing when the tops start dying back. Once they are finished growing, pull them all out, and cure them with the tops on for a few weeks in a cool, dry place. Top the dried shallots an inch above the bulb. At this point separate the shallots into individual cloves, like garlic, to make sure no moisture is left in the plant. You can expect them to keep in storage until the following spring.

VARIETIES 'Prisma' is an attractive reddish purple variety (seeds, not sets) that has worked well for me. A comparable variety in terms of color and growth habit is **'Camelot'**. **'Picasso'** sets are easy to grow and productive. Once you have grown a crop of shallots, you can always save bulbs from your harvest to plant again.

Spinach

Fresh, nutrient-rich spinach from your garden will be vastly different from the tasteless and slimy canned spinach that Popeye had to suffer through to get his muscles. Freshly wilted spinach with eggs or in soup, and spinach harvested at a baby size for salads are equally delicious. This is a fast and easy crop that you can have nearly all season in your garden.

GROWING For full-grown plants, sow 10 to 12 seeds per foot, about ½ inch deep, and cover with soil. For baby-sized spinach, sow 30 to 40 seeds a foot. In either case thinning is not necessary. Spinach requires fertile, moist soil. Amend the garden well and water in newly planted seeds. A moment of dryness when first planted will cause the seeds to go into permanent dormancy. Spinach will also germinate erratically when the soil temperature is over 80°F. Sometimes irrigation or shade cloth will help cool the soil enough to allow it to germinate.

HARVESTING For full-grown spinach, cut just above the soil when the leaves are 5 to 7 inches tall. For cut-and-come-again baby spinach, cut an inch above the soil; it will regrow a few times before it starts to bolt. This will be harder to accomplish in summer when spinach bolts easily.

VARIETIES 'Matador' has smooth, semi-savoyed leaves that are tender as either full-sized or baby spinach. I plant rich-tasting savoyed **'Bloomsdale Long Standing'** under shade cloth in summer because it is more resistant to bolting. **'Giant Winter'** is a good choice for cold hardiness and winter production in a hoop house.

Swiss Chard

Swiss chard's bold colors and rigid stems never cease to captivate me. The plants are both beautiful and delicious, making them an excellent addition to an edible landscape. With a distinctive flavor and good ability to hold up when cooked, Swiss chard has supplanted spinach in my kitchen for several dishes including soups and frittatas.

GROWING A planting of Swiss chard can last a few months. I usually plan for two successions per season, so that when the first planting gets tired, I have another one coming in. Chard prefers cooler weather, but it will push through the hotter summer months with proper irrigation. Start plants indoors 6 to 8 weeks before transplanting. Plant two or three seeds in a pot or cell, ½ inch deep, and cover with soil. Although chard is fairly hardy, deep frosts can damage young plants, so I wait until the threat of freezing has passed before transplanting. Transplant these clumps around 8 to 12 inches apart, with 12 to 18 inches between rows. This spacing will allow you to easily hoe between the plants and keep them weeded. Leaf miners and grasshoppers are occasionally problematic

for chard. Remove damaged leaves and toss them in your compost, allowing for new growth. If the problem persists, use a row cover for protection.

HARVESTING When the leaves are 8 to 12 inches long, begin harvesting the outside leaves by pinching or cutting the leaves off from the plant; be careful not to pull the plant out of the ground. Leave the center of the plant to continue producing. For the first harvest, I usually only take two or three leaves from each plant. Once it is mature, you can take four or five leaves from each plant but keep most of the plant intact, so it continues producing vigorously. Each time you harvest, remove damaged or old leaves from the plant.

VARIETIES **'Bright Lights'** produces gorgeous leaves in colors such as red, yellow, and white. For growers that want a little more red, I recommend **'Ruby Red'**. Another reliable variety is the white and green **'Fordhook Giant'**.

Tomatoes

My oldest son, Elijah, didn't like tomatoes for many years—until he encountered the small, yellow, pear variety that he was brave enough to try. He thought if he tried something new, it might change his mind. He was right. We have such strong perceptions of what we think we don't like to eat, but a little nudge can open up a whole new world. When I was a kid, heirloom tomatoes didn't exist, and fresh, sun-ripened tomatoes were just as rare. The variety and freshness now available are so compelling that hardly any effort is needed to convince people to give them a try. Tomatoes are vigorous plants that want to grow, and given great soil and adequate water, they will most likely thrive.

GROWING Sow seeds ⅛ inch deep in flats or cells, 6 to 8 weeks before you are going to transplant (ideally 1 or 2 weeks after last frost). Healthy tomato seedlings should be sturdy and short

rather than tall and leggy so don't start them too soon (and if you are purchasing transplants, avoid the mature ones). To encourage faster germination, use a heat mat or keep plants in a heated room so that soil warms to 75 to 90°F. Remove the heat mat once plants get going but continue growing transplants in a warm place with good light. Harden off plants slowly before planting by reducing water and fertilizer, and do not plant in the garden until nighttime temperatures are consistently above 50°F. Some growers use black plastic mulch to warm the soil, or row covers are a good idea, especially in colder areas.

In full sun and slightly acidic, rich soil, space plants 3 feet apart in rows 5 feet apart. Plant tomatoes so that the soil level is just below the lowest leaves. This way, roots will form along the buried stem and establish a stronger root system. All tomato plants need support, usually by a combination of stakes, cages, and twine, which should be set up at planting time. To reduce cracking, water evenly. Letting tomatoes completely dry out followed by heavy watering will cause the fruit to grow faster than the skin can handle.

A member of the nightshade family, the tomato is susceptible to several viral and bacterial problems. Copper and hydrogen peroxide (H_2O_2) work best as a preventative, so if you have had serious problems in the past, spray weekly when the plants begin to mature. If you already have a problem, these sprays might slow down a disease, but you won't get rid of it, because most of them spread by spores. Aphids tend to be problematic indoors, but in a hot, dry July garden, they usually won't bother tomatoes. And as long as there aren't too many of them, they won't affect fruit production anyway. Hornworms, on the other hand, can wreak havoc. At the first signs of munched-on plants (or fruit), start searching; they won't be far from the damage. Dispose of any you find on the plant. Removing suckers—which grow between the main vine and the branch and do nothing but sap energy—keeps the tomato plant focused on producing fruit. Pruning allows for air movement, which helps with disease prevention, and makes it easier to see and harvest ripe fruits. Always dip your sharp knife or pruner in bleach or H_2O_2 before pruning, and if you suspect that any of your plants are diseased, clean your cutting tool between plants as well. Diseases spread easily enough from plant to plant on their own, so don't help them out. As plants mature, feel free to train vines out of your paths and in the direction you want them to grow. They will quickly adjust. If they continue to grow in the unwanted direction, just keep moving them. If you are growing vines vertically, you can train them to spread out nicely on the trellis too.

HARVESTING Harvest tomatoes when the sun is out and the dew has dried (diseases spread more easily when plants are wet). You can generally tell if a tomato is ripe when it reaches its full color and begins to feel a little soft. Some heirlooms that are considered white or green can be a little tricky visually, but you'll quickly learn what a ripe one feels like. Unlike most hybrid red tomatoes, heirlooms don't have much shelf life. If you aren't going to eat them all right away, pull them off the vine a day or two early when they still have some firmness.

VARIETIES For red tomatoes, **'Big Beef'** is probably the most popular hybrid variety grown in North America. They have good disease resistance, they are just the right size for a sandwich, and they produce well. You could also try the heirloom classic **'Beefsteak'**. A moderately sized red tomato that also has good disease resistance is the heirloom **'Rutgers'**. One of my favorite heirloom tomatoes is **'Ananas Noire'** (also known as black pineapple) simply because of its outstanding flavor. Other excellent heirlooms are **'Brandywine'** (pink), **'White Tomesol'** (white), **'Tasty Evergreen'** (green), **'Cherokee Purple'** (black), and **'Striped German'** (orange). One of the earliest tomatoes you can grow is **'Glacier'**, a small red tomato packed with flavor. For sauce tomatoes try **'San Marzano'**. They are big, and the fruit is dry, meaning it takes less time to cook them down for sauce. When it comes to cherry tomatoes, pound for pound, nothing beats **'Sungold'**. They are sweeter than any other cherry tomato, but they do split easily, so be gentle when harvesting. **'Snow White'** is an heirloom cherry tomato with a surprising color and a delicate flavor. Don't stop with this list though, dive into your catalogs, and pick a few new ones to try each year.

Turnips

Growing salad turnips has changed my relationship to turnips forever. I used to know turnips only as a rustic fall crop that could withstand months in dark storage. They are especially good roasted, and the greens go well with bacon, but I wouldn't have counted them among the crops that I eagerly anticipate every year. But salad turnips are in a category all their own: sweet, tender, and just as good raw as they are cooked. So, if you think you don't like turnips, give salad turnips a chance.

GROWING Turnips grow well from seed and like most root crops they are not good candidates for transplanting. Generally, turnips take around 50 days to mature. You can grow them in the spring and then plant another patch in midsummer for fall harvesting. As soon as soil is workable, sow approximately 25 seeds per foot for small salad turnips, and 10 to 12 seeds per foot for larger turnips. Plant seeds ½ inch deep and cover with soil. Thin when greens are large enough to use, spacing 1 inch between small turnips and 2 inches between large turnips. To avoid the two main turnip issues—flea beetles on the greens and root maggots—place a row cover over the plants before they emerge from the soil.

HARVESTING Most large turnips are ready when the roots are baseball-size, around 3 inches in diameter. Salad turnips are perfect at the size of a golf ball. Once they mature, gently pull them out of the ground, cut off and rinse the tops, and scrub the root.

VARIETIES The standard salad turnip is the hybrid **'Hakurei'**, but I also enjoy **'Tokinashi'**. Both are tender, sweet with a little spiciness, and the greens are tender as well. A more traditional turnip, **'Gold Ball'** has smooth flesh and a nutty flavor. Classic heirloom **'Purple Top White Globe'** can grow up to 6 inches in diameter and still be good. It will store for months, so it's perfect for those dead-of-winter soups.

Winter Squash

As one of the three sisters—a traditional, Indigenous method of growing that also includes corn and beans—squash is essential in the garden. Although it takes a lot of space to grow, it is a welcome fall treat, and can be stored all winter.

GROWING All squash are tender tropical plants easily damaged by frost, so don't plant until after the danger of frost has passed. Pre-warming the soil with black plastic mulch in zones 4 and 5 is helpful if you're comfortable using plastic in your garden. Start squash seeds indoors 3 or 4 weeks before your last frost date in 2- or 3-inch pots. Or direct sow 3 or 4 seeds, 1 or 2 inches deep, at the base of small mounds of soil spaced 4 to 6 feet apart. After plants leaf out, thin to one seedling per hill. As you plan your winter squash patch carefully consider the length of your season, as many varieties can take 120 days to fully ripen. Winter squash requires more space than summer squash. Generally speaking, the larger the fruit, the larger

the vine, so if you have limited space, choose a smaller-sized squash. Keep squash plants well watered, especially when fruiting.

HARVESTING The mature color of the fruit, which you will know from experience or from looking at pictures, is a good indicator of ripeness. Also, if your fingernail no longer easily dents the rind, the squash is ready to harvest. Carefully cut the fruits from the vine with pruners (it's a bigger job than most knives can handle). Leave a few inches of the stem on and avoid scratching or cutting the skin. After harvesting, allow the squash to cure in the sun for around 2 weeks to sweeten and deepen its flavor. Squash will store in a cool, dry place for a long time if it doesn't have any blemishes or ways for bacteria to get into the fruit. I advise wiping down the squash before storage (with H_2O_2, water, a vinegar solution, or bleach) to reduce the number of bacteria on the skin.

VARIETIES The list of varieties to choose from is seemingly endless, but here are my favorites for flavor, convenience, and a mix of colors. Butternut types, such as **'Waltham'** or **'Seminole Pumpkin'**, are the classic winter squash with excellent flavor and long storage. Delicata squash is compact, easy to roast, has edible skin, and is perfect stuffed. **'Zeppelin'** is excellent, but if you are short on space, a bush variety simply called **'Bush Delicata'** takes up less room. The gorgeous deep orange color of **'Red Kuri'** continues into the nutty and smooth flesh. A showstopper, **'Guatemalan Blue Banana'** is a huge, long fruit with mottled blue skin that tastes great too. **'Kikuza'** has a distinctive flavor that hints at chestnuts. Other varieties that are worth considering are **'Hubbard'**, **'Buttercup'**, and **'Carnival'**. For edible pumpkins, try **'New England Sugar Pie'** and russeted **'Winter Luxury'**. **'Howden'** is a 30-ish-pound, reliable carving pumpkin.

Zucchini and Summer Squash

After a few months of mostly green crops, I just love the color and substance of zucchini and summer squash. Their role is more supporting than lead, adding nuance and texture to many things we cook, but they are important nonetheless. It helps to choose more flavorful varieties and harvest them when small. In addition to the fruit, squash blossoms are edible and are especially fantastic when stuffed with cheese and fried. Yet another reason to grow squash.

GROWING Zucchini and summer squash have similar growth habits. Some varieties are more compact, but most need at least a 3-foot by 3-foot space. To stay ahead of weeds and pests, I start squash in 2- or 3-inch pots and transplant them after soil has warmed. At this point you can also direct sow, planting 3 to 5 seeds, about 1 to 2 inches deep, at the base of hills that are 3 feet apart. When the plants develop their first set of leaves, thin to 2 or 3 plants. Squash are susceptible to mildew, squash bugs, and vine borers, but if your plant is strong it will tolerate some pressure and produce quite a lot of fruit before these problems overcome it. Healthy soil, plenty of water, and enough room between plants for good air movement will go a long way.

HARVESTING Once plants begin producing, the fruit comes fast and furious: check your plants daily. Depending on the variety I like to harvest squash and zucchini around 6 to 10 inches, with zucchini being a little bigger. Larger fruits are still okay to eat, they will just have larger seeds; you can stuff them or use them to make bread. You can usually twist zucchini and summer squash from the plants, but if they don't come away easily use pruners or a small knife to cut them off. Rinse your harvest and scrub off any slime from the flower on the blossom end. Squash varieties generally have scratchy spines along the leaves and branches. For most people it is just an irritation, but if it really bothers you wear a long-sleeve shirt and gloves when harvesting. If you want to harvest squash blossoms, only harvest the male flowers. Squash produces more male flowers than they need, and you want to avoid stealing future fruit by taking the females. Male flowers grow on a longer stem, away from the center of the plant; female flowers grow closer to the plant and often have a discernable bulge at the base of the flower—this is the future fruit. Also, male flowers have only a single stamen at the center of the flower, whereas female flowers have a stigma with multiple stems in a circle around the center. Without being graphic, you could almost imagine how the parts fit together. To harvest the blossoms, snap or cut the male flower from its long stem. Blossoms are extremely fragile so keep refrigerated and use as soon as possible.

VARIETIES Varieties fall into three groups: summer squash, zucchini, and patty pan. **'Lemon'** is one of the most fun summer squashes to grow, hands down. It has a bright yellow color and is shaped just like a lemon. The classic **'Yellow Crookneck'** is always a reliable producer. **'Costata Romanesca'** is an Italian heirloom zucchini with deep ridges in the flesh, a mottled green skin, and a rich flavor. If you are short on space, **'Astia'** has a smaller bushlike growth habit and produces tons of dark green, uniform zucchini. This variety can even be grown in containers. Of the patty pan squash, which resemble spaceships and are mostly used at a baby size, my favorite is the beautiful yellow **'Golden Custard'**. Patty pan grow even faster than other summer squash and zucchini, so stay on top of harvesting them.

RESOURCES

SEEDS AND PLANTS

Baker Creek Heirloom Seed Company
2278 Baker Creek Road
Mansfield, MO 65704
www.rareseeds.com
Offers a wide selection of unique and heirloom seeds from around the world. They also produce an incredible seed catalog filled with seed stories, varietal histories, recipes, and grower profiles.

True Love Seeds
PO Box 12648
Philadelphia, PA 19129˙
www.trueloveseeds.com
A farm-based seed company offering culturally important and open-pollinated vegetable, herb, and flower seeds.

Seed Savers Exchange
3094 North Winn Road
Decorah, IA 52101
www.seedsavers.org
A wonderful nonprofit dedicated to preserving heirloom seeds. They also have a member organization through which you can exchange seeds with other growers.

High Mowing Seeds
76 Quarry Road
Wolcott, VT 05680
www.highmowingseeds.com
The source for Certified Organic vegetable seed. They also produce a lot of their own seeds.

Johnny's Selected Seeds
13 Main Street
Fairfield, ME 04937
www.johnnyseeds.com
Johnny's offers an informative catalog with lots of charts and instructions, and they carry a good selection of growing supplies and tools.

Fedco Seeds
PO Box 520
Waterville, ME 04903
www.fedcoseeds.com
They produce a well-written informative catalog geared toward northern growers, and they support small seed producers when possible.

Krieger's Nursery
9555 N. Gast Road
Bridgman, MI 49106
www.berryplants.com
Mail-order source for several types of small fruiting plants, as well as some perennials like rhubarb and hop rhizomes.

Seeds from Italy
PO Box 3908
Lawrence, KS 66046
www.growitalian.com
Authentic Italian seeds imported from Italy, including some amazing sauce tomato varieties that are hard to find anywhere else.

Wood Prairie Farm
49 Kinney Road
Bridgewater, ME 04735
www.woodprairie.com
Great source of high-quality potato seed with a wide selection of delicious varieties.

TOOLS AND SUPPLIES

Greenhouse Megastore
1644 Georgetown Road
Danville, IL 61832
www.greenhousemegastore.com
Seller of high-quality heat mats, lights, and other seed-starting supplies. Their knowledgeable staff engineers will patiently assist you with setting up a small hoop house or greenhouse.

Peaceful Valley Farm Supply
125 Clydesdale Court
Grass Valley, CA 95945
www.groworganic.com
Peaceful Valley has been supplying organic farmers and gardeners since 1976. A great source for well-priced seeds and other gardening supplies.

Morgan Composting
4353 US 10
Sears, MI 49679
www.dairydoo.com
The makers of Dairy Doo and other fine garden products. Hands down the best fertilizer I have ever used.

SOIL TESTING

CSI: Crop Services International
29246 Lake St.
Marcellus, MI 49067
www.cropservicesintl.com
A top-notch service if you are looking for nuanced and insightful recommendations for amending your garden, building your soil, and troubleshooting. They are more geared toward professional growers, but they will test anyone's soil.

Michigan State University Extension
msue.anr.msu.edu/resources/soil_test_kit_self-mailer
This is a cost-effective way to get basic soil testing done for your garden. Extension agents can be hit or miss. If you are not sure you are getting the best advice, try someone else.

FURTHER READING

Cobb, Tanya Denckla. 2003. *The Gardener's A–Z Guide to Growing Organic Food.* **North Adams, Massachusetts: Storey Publishing, LLC.**
I love this book for the alphabetical layout of vegetable plants. I keep it handy to quickly reference spacing, companion plants, root depth, and more.

Cranshaw, Whitney, and David Shetlar. 2017. *Garden Insects of North America: The Ultimate Guide to Backyard Bugs, 2nd edition.* **Princeton, New Jersey: Princeton University Press.**
If you want to become an expert on the hundreds of insects you will encounter as a gardener, this is *the* guide. It is comprehensive and accurate with great photos and descriptions.

Harstad, Carolyn. 1999. *Go Native!: Gardening with Native Plants and Wildflowers in the Lower Midwest.* **Bloomington, Indiana: Indiana University Press.**
Learning about native plants is a worthwhile journey that could have a huge benefit for your vegetable garden. If you want to transition the landscaping around your house to native plants, this is a great guide.

Weaver, William Woys. 2018. *Heirloom Vegetable Gardening: A Master Gardener's Guide to Planting, Seed Saving, and Cultural History.* **Beverly, Massachusetts: Voyageur Press.**
Filled with beautiful photos, this book will introduce you to the world of heirloom plants. Weaver has a deep understanding of the history of these plants, and includes many useful details for both the garden and the kitchen.

Martin, Deborah L., Fern Marshall Bradley, Barbara W. Ellis, and Ellen Phillips. 2017. *Rodale's Ultimate Enyclopedia of Organic Gardening: The Indispensable Green Resource for Every Gardener.* **New York: Rodale Books.**
This comprehensive book, with advice ranging from compost to garden pests, is a great reference tool for any gardener.

Logsdon, Gene. 1983. *Gene Logsdon's Wildlife in Your Garden: Or Dealing with Deer, Rabbits, Raccoons, Moles, Crows, Sparrows, and Other of Nature's Creatures.* **New York: Rodale Press.**
Logsdon has a wise, grandfatherly tone and a welcome, practical approach to nature, farming, gardening, and other topics. He is also the author of several other worthwhile books including *Holy Shit* and *Living at Nature's Pace*, which I found particularly moving.

Coleman, Eliot. 2009.*The Winter Harvest Handbook: Year-Round Vegetable Production Using Deep-Organic Techniques and Unheated Greenhouses.* **White River Junction, Vermont: Chelsea Green Publishing.**

If you like technology, innovation, and down-to-earth advice, Eliot is your guy. He has been trying to figure out how to make his 2-acre plot as productive as possible for the past few decades through listening to nature, innovative tools, and intelligent pest control. Although Coleman has been influential in the organic farming world, he grows more on the scale of a gardener.

MY FAVORITE COOKBOOKS

Sherman, Sean, with Beth Dooley. 2017. *The Sioux Chef's Indigenous Kitchen.* **Minneapolis: University of Minnesota.**

An amazing book about Indigenous ingredients and cuisine. A must-have book for any gardener, chef, or lover of food.

Perelman, Deb. 2012. *The Smitten Kitchen Cookbook.* **New York: self-published.**

This innovative cook works in a tiny New York City kitchen, and eschews pretentious ingredients. Her style is approachable, and she focuses on fresh, seasonal ingredients.

Swanson, Heidi. 2011. *Super Natural Everyday.* **Berkely: Ten Speed Press.**

Hailing from San Francisco, Swanson focuses her recipes on nutrient-dense whole ingredients that she teaches you how to use. This vegetarian cookbook is full of gorgeous photographs that will inspire you to use your vegetables in new ways.

Madison, Deborah. 1997. *Vegetarian Cooking for Everyone.* **New York: Broadway Books.**

This is the vegetarian cooking bible. The great thing is that it is not dogmatic, as many of the recipes work with meat, and she explores that on occasion. This book is as useful for a new cook as it is for someone experienced in the kitchen.

PLANT HARDINESS ZONES

ZONE	TEMPERATURE (°F)		
1	Below −50		
2	−50	to	−40
3	−40	to	−30
4	−30	to	−20
5	−20	to	−10
6	−10	to	0
7	0	to	10
8	10	to	20
9	20	to	30
10	30	to	40
11	40	to	50
12	50	to	60
13	60	to	70

PHOTOGRAPHY AND ILLUSTRATION CREDITS

PHOTOGRAPHY

Alamy
Tony Watson: 126

Jackie Connelly: 141

GAP Photos
Gary Smith: 42

Marie Iannotti: 154, 193

iStockphoto
Scharfsinn86: 2–3; jmsilva: 8–9; Atom Studios: 18; space-monkey-pics: 30; BruceBlock: 33; IPGGutenbergUKLtd: 62; YuriyS: 67; Cynthia Shirk: 77; Ken Wiedemann: 78; kosobu: 87; Jetanat: 90; JPrescott: 94; ejkrouse: 98; wwing: 138; Pavliha: 144–145; valvirga: 152; sagarmanis: 156; CreativeFire: 157; Eugenegg: 160; efilippou: 162; KChodorowski: 163; TasiPas: 167; duckycards: 179; johnnyscriv: 182; moisseyev: 184; Volodymyr Kyrylyuk: 185; Zoya2222: 186; JeffKontur: 187; Mindstyle: 188; zeleno: 194

Pixabay
858106: 153; evitaochel: 189; BabaMu: 190

PxHere
Used under a Creative Commons Zero (CC0) License: 50, 72, 158, 160, 164, 171, 172, 173, 174, 176, 180, 181

Shutterstock
Phil Darby: 16; Fabio Pagani: 21; Rainer Fuhrmann: 22; Boumen Japet: 28; Del Boy: 35; jkcDesign: 36; Rawpixel.com: 41; Michelle Lee Photography: 46; Skeronov: 48; Ulza: 82; Nadzeya Pakhomav: 93; Alexander Raths: 102; Miyuki Satake: 107; mcajan: 109; Grandiflora 110; mnimage: 114; Rawpixel 118; Iuliia Karnaushenko: 132; vitec: 136; Marchenko Olga: 166; Denis Pogostin: 170; New Africa: 183; Venkat Parkunan: 192

Wikimedia Commons
Used under a Creative Commons Attribution–Share Alike 4.0 International Public License
Michael Barera: 10

Used under a Creative Commons Attribution–Share Alike 3.0 Unported license
Jamain: 159, 169

Used under a Creative Commons Attribution–Share Alike 2.0 Generic license
H. Alexander Talbot: 168

Released into the Public Domain
Preston Keres, USDA: 40–41; Maria Chantal Rodriguez Nilsson: 123; Stephen Ausmus, USDA ARS: 178

ILLUSTRATIONS

David Deis/Dreamline Cartography: 13

iStockphoto
rubinat: 5; aqua_marinka: 41, 113; kateja: 53, 59

Juliana Johnson: 88

Julia Sadler: 23, 26, 29, 38, 55, 57, 68, 69 70, 79, 81, 100, 101, 108, 116, 124

Shutterstock
maritime_m: 7, 9, 12, 20, 32, 84, 97; 144–145; Ann Doronina: 75; ArtMari: 91, 191; sdp_creations: 199

INDEX

delicata squash, 193

diatomaceous earth (DE), 89

digging forks, 54, 56, 66

dinosaur kale, 171

direct sowing of seeds. *See also plant profiles in* Edibles A to Z *section*

   in fall season, 119, 120

   in spring season, 65, 74, 75, 85

   in summer season, 96, 104

disease control, 33–34, 39, 84, 86–89, 96, 135. *See also plant profiles in* Edibles A to Z *section*

diversity of plants, 22, 33, 76

drip irrigation, 28

Drummer soil, 25

dry beans, 154, 155

Dutch white clover, 108–109

E

earwigs, 89

earworm, 164, 165, 181

edge habitats, 76

eggplant, 167

eggplant, varieties of

   'Black Beauty', 167

   'Casper', 167

   'Listada de Gandia', 167

   'Pingtung Long', 167

electric fence systems, 90

endive, 183

English peas, 180

ephemerals, 76

extension service, and preservation information, 115

F

Facebook, and garden photos, 39

fall armyworm, 181

fall season, 104, 114, 119–137, 173

Farmers' Almanac website, 12

farmers' markets, 83, 91

fava beans, 168

fava beans, varieties of

   'Aquadulce', 168

   'Sweet Lorane', 168

   'Vroma', 168

   'Windsor', 168

February garden activities, 51–61

fencing, 64, 89–90

fennel, 169

fennel, varieties of

   'Orion', 169

   'Zefa Fino', 169

fertilizers, 22–24. *See also plant profiles in* Edibles A to Z *section*

   for bare-root plants, 80

   for containers, 37

   and journal entries, 39

   with organic mulches, 93

   for seedlings, 59, 69

   side-dressing with, 116

field corn, 164

fingerling potatoes, 182

firmness of vegetables, to determine ripeness, 98–99

flavor of vegetables, to determine ripeness, 99

flea beetles, 86, 152, 157, 167, 172, 184, 192

Florence fennel, 169

Florida weave technique, 101

flour corn, 165

flowers, ephemeral, 76

Focus: HOPE project, 41

forests, 76

Frederik Meijer Gardens, 11

frost. *See also plant profiles in* Edibles A to Z *section*

   and frost-free window, 17

   frost tolerance chart, 130

   and garden journals, 128

   impact of first frost, 129–131, 133

   Michigan frost dates chart, 14

   and microclimates, 14–15

   protection from, 70–71, 85, 125

   resources, 12

fruit crops, 15, 34, 44, 80–81, 131

frying peppers, 181

fungicides, 89, 159, 184

G

garages for harvest storage, 122, 131, 170

garden cleanup, 135

garden design and planning, 31–39, 43–49, 96

   for fall garden, 104, 112, 114

   in fall season, 127–128, 134

   and journal entries, 39, 64, 112

   for winter garden, 112

   in winter season, 139–142

gardening, about, 19–20

garden journals, 39

   in fall season, 120, 128, 134

   in spring season, 64, 74

   in winter season, 44, 142

garden mapping, 44, 47–48

garden reflections, 141–142

garden teepees, 79, 155

HEATHER COHEN

Bevin Cohen is an author, herbalist, gardener, seed saver, and educator. He is the owner of Small House Farm and the founder of Michigan Seed Library Network, a community seed sharing initiative that has helped establish more than one hundred seed library programs. Bevin offers workshops and lectures across the country on the benefits of living closer to the land through seeds, herbs, and locally grown food and he has written a number of books on these topics, including *Saving Our Seeds*, *The Artisan Herbalist*, and *The Complete Guide to Seed & Nut Oils*. Learn more about Bevin's work at www.smallhousefarm.com.